Smoking Cessation

European Respiratory Monograph 42
December 2008

Editor in Chief
K. Larsson

This book is one in a series of European Respiratory Monographs. Each individual issue provides a comprehensive overview of one specific clinical area of respiratory health, communicating information about the most advanced techniques and systems needed to investigate it. It provides factual and useful scientific detail, drawing on specific case studies and looking into the diagnosis and management of individual patients. Previously published titles in this series are listed at the back of this book with details of how they can be purchased.

Smoking Cessation

Edited by
S. Nardini

European Respiratory
Society

Published by European Respiratory Society Journals Ltd ©2008
December 2008
Hardback ISBN: 978-1-904097-63-1
Paperback ISBN: 978-1-904097-64-8
ISSN: 1025-448x
Printed by Latimer Trend & Co. Ltd, Plymouth, UK

Business matters (enquiries, advertisement bookings) should be addressed to: European Respiratory
Society Journals Ltd, Publications Office, 442 Glossop Road, Sheffield, S10 2PX, UK.
Tel: 44 114 2672860; Fax: 44 114 2665064; E-mail: Monograph@ersj.org.uk

The European Respiratory Monograph

Number 42   December 2008

CONTENTS

The Guest Editor

S. Nardini

The Guest Editor

S. Nardini graduated in 1976 in Padua where he gained his speciality in Chest Medicine (1979) and History of Medicine (1986). He was Head of the Pulmonary Rehabilitation and Intermediate Intensive Care Unit of the Morelli Hospital in Sondalo (1994–1996) after which he became Head of the Pulmonary and Tuberculosis Unit in Vittorio, Venete. The post he still holds today.

Since the early 1990s he has collaborated on many international working groups including: CARG (the Coordination Advise and Review Group) of the World Health Organization (WHO-Geneva); Scientific Committee on Tobacco and Health in the International Union Against Tuberculosis and Lung Disease; the Society for Research on Nicotine and Tobacco; The European Respiratory Society's Working Group Tobacco, Smoking Control and Health Education. The AIPO-Italian National Thoracic Society's Prevention and Health Education (Tobacco Control) Working Group. He also started the Italian National Project for Smoke-Free Hospitals.

He is currently the advisor for the Tobacco Related Health Problems for the National Institute of Health (Instituto Superiore di Santità-Roma). He participated in the coordination of the "smoke-free hospitals" within the Veneto Regional Government (2003–2005). He is currently responsible for the area of "Smoking Cessation" and the "Smoking Cessation Clinic" network and strongly involved in the Global Alliance against Chronic Respiratory Diseases (GARD) of the WHO in Italy.

He has held several editorial positions including: editorial office manager of the journal *Multidisciplinary Respiratory Medicine*; is part of the editorial board of the Italian edition of the *American Journal Of Respiratory and Critical Care Medicine* and the *Italian Journal Of Chest Diseases*. He is also the author of over 300 scientific abstracts and papers.

Preface

Smoking has been practised for more than 7,000 years and is today the most common form of drug abuse worldwide. The use of tobacco seems to have started in South America and was brought to Europe in the 16th century and was, after that, spread out into most major societies within the next 100 years. Today, there are more than one billion smokers worldwide. There is no doubt that smoking poses the greatest single individual risk factor for premature death. It is alarming to note that, among the five highest risk factors for premature death in 2020, four are closely related to tobacco smoking. It is with sadness, but not surprise, that one can establish the fact that two of these four causes, chronic obstructive pulmonary disease and lung cancer, are to be found within the field of pulmonary medicine. Based on this, one of the most important tasks for preventive medicine is to fight and try to defeat the use of tobacco smoking. Therefore, it is of utmost importance to take measures that will ensure young people will not start smoking. However, this is much a matter of lifestyle and may not, primarily, be a task for medical healthcare professionals, but rather for parents and other adults, nonsmokers serving as models, the school and the society in general. It is, however, an important task for medical healthcare to help those who have commenced smoking to stop their abuse. This task extends over all specialities both in the medical and surgical fields. This makes the book you have in front of you so important and recommendable to all colleagues, irrespective of speciality.

It is, therefore, a pleasure to introduce this *European Respiratory Monograph* on Smoking Cessation to European Respiratory Society members and other healthcare professionals who want to help patients who have not yet stopped smoking. The book is written by experts in the field and has a wide focus on different aspects of smoking cessation, and I am certain it will find its way and be of help to many care providers who meet smokers in daily life.

K. Larsson
Editor in Chief

Eur Respir Mon, 2008, 42, ix. Printed in UK - all rights reserved. Copyright ERS Journals Ltd 2008; European Reapiratory Monograph; ISSN 1025-448x.

CHAPTER 1

European Respiratory Society activities for a smoke-free Europe

G. Viegi,#, L. Carrozzi#,¶, F. Pistelli#,¶*

National Research Council Institute of Biomedicine and Molecular Immunology, Palermo, and #Pulmonary Environmental Epidemiology Unit, National Research Council Institute of Clinical Physiology, and ¶Cardio-Thoracic Dept, University Hospital of Pisa, Pisa, Italy.

Correspondence: G. Viegi, National Research Council Institute of Biomedicine and Molecular Immunology, Via U. La Malfa, 153, 90146 Palermo, Italy. Fax: 39 0916809122; E-mail: viegi@ibim.cnr.it

General context

Comprehensive smoke-free legislation is spreading in Europe. Lithuania, Iceland, France, the UK and Spain recently joined Ireland, Norway, Italy, Malta, Cyprus and Sweden in introducing a smoking ban in public places [1]. The European Network for Smoking Prevention (ENSP) periodically provides an updated summary of the latest developments regarding smoke-free workplace legislation in Europe [2].

The European Respiratory Society (ERS) has contributed greatly, since its foundation in 1990, to dissemination of awareness of the health risks of smoking and the need and possibility of doctors helping smokers willing to quit, and by reinforcing the need for a smoke-free Europe [3, 4].

ERS structure regarding tobacco problems

Indeed, it is remarkable that a largely clinically oriented society has decided to have a scientific working group devoted to the public health aspects of smoking cessation and control, Working Group 06.03 (Tobacco, Smoking Control & Health Education), which forms part of Assembly 6 (Occupation and Epidemiology). This group has shown annual increases in membership and scientific quantity and quality, as reflected by the congress programmes, with well-attended symposia and postgraduate courses, as well as numerous publications in the *European Respiratory Journal* [5–11].

Moreover, in the latter half of the 1990s, a growing ERS identified advocacy as a third pillar within the domain of a medical society, beyond but linked to science and education. Then, an *ad hoc* committee, named the Smoking Prevention Committee, was formed, which has now become the Tobacco Control Committee. This Committee has been of great importance, together with the ERS Brussels office, and in collaboration with the European Lung Foundation (ELF), in setting the agenda for the public anti-tobacco activities of the ERS towards governmental and parliamentary institutions at the European level [12].

Eur Respir Mon, 2008, 42, 1–7. Printed in UK - all rights reserved. Copyright ERS Journals Ltd 2008; European Respiratory Monograph; ISSN 1025-448x.

Collaborative European Anti-Smoking Evaluation study

A pioneering activity of Assembly 6, at the time led by Paolo Paoletti, in promoting the spread of smoking cessation clinics was the Collaborative European Anti-Smoking Evaluation (CEASE) study, a multicentric study that permitted the ERS to take an important step towards the promotion of European research in pulmonary medicine [13, 14].

The CEASE trial was based on a randomised double-blind parallel-group study design, and performed in 17 countries all over Europe; 36 chest clinics enrolled 3,575 smokers from the general population. The main objective was to evaluate whether or not sustained abstinence from cigarette smoking for 1 yr could be increased by using higher-than-standard doses (25 versus 15 mg) of nicotine patch, and/or prolonging the treatment period (26 versus 12 weeks). The trial confirmed the efficacy of nicotine patches in improving smoking cessation rates, particularly using higher-than-standard doses [14]. Analyses of the variation in respiratory symptoms and lung function, performed at baseline and after 1 yr, provided objective measurements of the beneficial effects of smoking cessation, as well as the potential usefulness of spirometric evaluation in smoking cessation [15, 16]. The trial yielded further information for fostering the implementation of smoking cessation programmes [17]. For example, using the methodological tools assessed in the CEASE trial, the Smoking Cessation Clinic of the Cardio-Thoracic Dept of Pisa University Hospital (Pisa, Italy) was founded. The trial's experience [13, 14] has been carried out in smoking outpatients from the general population [18], and this standardised approach has permitted the analysis of results and critical aspects of smoking cessation in a real-life setting [19]. Recently, this physician-assisted smoking cessation programme has been also applied within the framework of a randomised study on lung cancer screening using low-dose computed tomography [20], and, to date, has shown promising results in terms of smoking cessation in this selected population of smokers [21]. In general, smoking cessation centres implemented in pulmonary clinics represent a cornerstone for the development of different preventive and therapeutic interventions against smoking-related problems.

ERS *European Lung White Book*

To date, the most important advocacy activity carried out by the ERS, in collaboration with the ELF, has been the publication of the *European Lung White Book. The First Comprehensive Survey on Respiratory Health in Europe* [22]. This book, edited by former presidents and senior officers of the ERS, was produced through a collective society effort, and was launched on November 25, 2003 at the European Parliament in Brussels in the presence of the then European Commissioner David Byrne. Part 3 of the book covers the major risk factors for respiratory diseases, *i.e.* tobacco smoking and environmental risk factors. In particular, it provides information on the trends in smoking prevalence, tobacco taxation and social costs from tobacco use, as well as on the links of several respiratory diseases with active and passive smoking.

A reduced version of the *European Lung White Book* has been translated into several languages and disseminated among several stakeholders at national levels. It has surely contributed to spreading knowledge of ERS scientific, educational and advocacy activities, for the sake of European pulmonary patients.

The ERS is now working on the publication of a second edition within a few years in order to be ready to face the challenges of the next decade.

European Commission Analysis of the Science and Policy for European Control of Tobacco report

Subsequently, in 2004, Fiona Godfrey, the European Union (EU) Policy Advisor of the ERS, within the Analysis of the Science and Policy for European Control of Tobacco (ASPECT) Consortium, collaborated with the European Commission (EC) to publish the report *Tobacco or Health in the European Union. Past, Present and Future* [23].

This comprehensive booklet covers: tobacco use and effects on health; the economics of tobacco and tobacco control in the EU; the development of EU tobacco-control policy; the impact of tobacco-control policy on smoking in the EU; tobacco product regulation; and the influence of the tobacco industry on European tobacco-control policy. Finally, the recommendations point out the investment and regulatory capacity from the organisational and structural side; the need for greater research capacity; and specific smoking prevention interventions.

ERS Smoke-free Europe 2005

Importantly, the ERS co-organised a Smoke Free Europe Conference in Luxembourg, on June 2, 2005 [24]. It occurred during the meeting of the European Health Council. Opened by the Minister of Health of Luxembourg, it was a unique occasion for discussing the need to act for the protection of the health of workers and the general public with the Health Ministers of countries that had introduced or were planning to introduce a smoking ban: Ireland, Italy, Sweden, Finland, Latvia, Poland, Malta, Hungary, and Cyprus. The conference participants also heard the view of the European Parliament, and the closing keynote addressed was made by the EU Director-General for Health and Consumer Protection.

ERS Research Seminar

Within this context, Working Group 06.03 (Tobacco, Smoking Control & Health Education) and the Tobacco Control Committee organised an ERS Research Seminar on Tobacco Control: Harm Reduction Strategies in Ferney Voltaire (France), on October 3–4, 2005 [25]. There were presentations on: the role of nicotine in cigarette-related morbidity; the role of the other components of cigarette smoke in cigarette-related morbidity; mechanisms and models of nicotine addiction in animals; tobacco smoking as an addiction; what is harm reduction (from outside tobacco smoking); "less-harmful" cigarettes and new cigarette substitutes; smoke-free tobacco; nicotine replacement therapy; the concept of recreational clean addictive nicotine; possible gains and risks; the regulatory framework; help from marketing; and proposals for the future.

It was an important occasion for scientifically discussing a controversial issue, important from a public health perspective, on which further studies in different parts of Europe are clearly needed before any general position can be taken.

ERS Lifting the Smokescreen

The 2006 report on passive smoking [26], presented to the European Parliament by the Smoke Free Partnership (the ERS, Cancer Research UK, the French National

Cancer Institute and the European Heart Network), estimated that, each year, passive smoking kills 79,000 people in the EU. In addition, it covered: the economics of smoke-free policies; the economic impact of a smoking ban in bars; public attitudes to smoke-free policies in Europe; why ventilation is not a viable alternative to a complete smoking ban; smoke-free success in Europe, mistakes made and lessons learnt; and the Limassol recommendations for obtaining comprehensive smoke-free legislation.

From a health education perspective, it is important that the reported 10 reasons for lifting the smokescreen are known and disseminated: 1) second-hand smoke exposure kills and harms health; 2) every worker has the right to be protected from exposure to tobacco smoke; 3) scientific evidence shows that ventilation does not protect against exposure to tobacco smoke; 4) smoke free laws do not result in negative economic effects; 5) freedom of choice includes the responsibility not to harm others; 6) the public supports smoke free legislation; 7) the public complies with smoke free legislation; 8) it has been done elsewhere, it can be done everywhere; 9) it is a cost effective public health intervention; and 10) comprehensive smoke free policies work.

ERS Task Force

Meanwhile, Working Group 06.03 (Tobacco, Smoking Control & Health Education) and Assembly 6 (Occupation and Epidemiology) decided to work hard, in collaboration with the Society for Research on Nicotine and Tobacco (SRNT), in setting out updated recommendations on smoking cessation to be applied within the usual care provided by pulmonary units in Europe.

The ERS Task Force document "Smoking cessation in patients with respiratory diseases: a high priority, integral component of therapy" was published in the *European Respiratory Journal* in 2007 [27].

This document involves a comprehensive review of different aspects of smoking and smoking cessation: epidemiology, tobacco/nicotine addiction, characteristics of patients who smoke, psychological and behavioural interventions, pharmacological treatment, organisational anchorage and education, and the costs of smoking and economics of smoking cessation. Seven key points briefly synthesise the main assessments and recommendations. All of the specific topics focus on patients with respiratory diseases in order to set standards in this area, ensure that pulmonary physicians act accordingly, and implement a scientific approach towards smoking cessation in this population. A final chapter on research prospects emphasises the need for additional efforts in this area. The highlighted investigation's main points are: treatments (in terms of both new pharmacological drugs and new/different management of established therapy), mechanism of tobacco dependence and motivation to quit, smoking reduction and smokeless products, comorbidity, research into more cost-effective approaches to smoking cessation tailored to respiratory patients.

European Respiratory Monograph

In this context, the initiative of S. Nardini in preparing an issue of the *European Respiratory Monograph* on smoking cessation should be appraised. It could be argued that the present Monograph appears too soon after the Task Force recommendations [27]. However, in this rapidly innovating field, 2 yrs may be a sufficient lag for updating procedures or describing the outcomes of new trials with new pharmacological treatments.

In addition, in order to achieve the goal that, in patients with respiratory diseases, smoking cessation genuinely becomes an integral component of therapy, the Latin expression *repetita iuvant* [repetition is useful] might even be welcome.

Summary

The ERS has contributed greatly to the dissemination of the awareness of the health risks of smoking, the need and possibility of doctors helping smokers to quit, and the need for a smoke-free Europe.

Working Group 06.03 (Tobacco, Smoking Control & Health Education), devoted to the scientific coverage of smoking cessation and control, has been increasing in membership and scientific quantity and quality in recent years. The *ad hoc* committee created by the ERS Executive Committee (the Tobacco Control Committee) is involved in advocacy. The ERS directly managed a multicentric randomised study (CEASE), performed in 17 European countries, which permitted an important step to be taken towards the promotion of research and implementation of smoking cessation programmes in clinical practice. Working Group 06.03, along with the Tobacco Control Committee, organised an ERS Research Seminar on Tobacco Control: Harm Reduction Strategies in 2005; this is a controversial issue, important from a public health perspective. The ERS co-organised a Smoke-free Europe conference in Luxembourg during the meeting of the European Health Council.

Relevant publications have been edited by the ERS: 1) the *European Lung White Book. The First Comprehensive Survey on Respiratory Health in Europe* (in collaboration with the ELF); 2) the report *Tobacco or Health in the European Union. Past, Present and Future* (in collaboration with the European Commission); 3) *Lifting the Smokescreen*, a report on passive smoking, presented to the European Parliament by the Smoke Free Partnership (ERS and other allies); 4) the updated recommendations on smoking cessation to be applied in pulmonary units in Europe (produced in collaboration with the Society for Research on Nicotine and Tobacco); and 5) the present issue of the *European Respiratory Monograph* on smoking cessation.

Such ERS activity can help pulmonary doctors to implement smoking cessation programmes, one of the most cost-effective public health activities.

Keywords: European Respiratory Society, second-hand smoke, smoking cessation.

References

1. World Health Organization. Who Report on the Global Tobacco Epidemic, 2008: the MPOWER Package. Geneva, World Health Organization, 2008.
2. European Network for Smoking Prevention. European Trends Towards Smoke-Free Provisions. www.ensp.org/files/legislation_on_smokefree_workplaces_200801.pdf Date last updated: January 2008. Date last accessed: 1 October 2008.
3. European Respiratory Society. European Respiratory Society. http://dev.ersnet.org
4. Nardini S, Zuccaro P, Viegi G. The smoking ban in Italy: lights and shadows after one year. *ERS Newsletter* July 2006; p. 11.

5. Paoletti P, Fornai E, Maggiorelli F, *et al.* Importance of baseline cotinine plasma values in smoking cessation: results from a double-blind study with nicotine patch. *Eur Respir J* 1996; 9: 643–651.

6. Tønnesen P, Mikkelsen KL, Markholst C, *et al.* Nurse-conducted smoking cessation with minimal intervention in a lung clinic: a randomized controlled study. *Eur Respir J* 1996; 9: 2351–2355.

7. Nardini S, Bertoletti R, Rastelli V, Donner CF. The influence of personal tobacco smoking on the clinical practice of Italian chest physicians. *Eur Respir J* 1998; 12: 1450–1453.

8. Jiménez-Ruiz C, Florez S, Ramos A, Ramos L, Solano S, Fornies E. Smoking cessation with a 16 h nicotine patch: results in a group of hospital workers. *Eur Respir J* 1997; 10: 573–575.

9. Jiménez-Ruiz C, Kunze M, Fagerström KO. Nicotine replacement: a new approach to reducing tobacco-related harm. *Eur Respir J* 1998; 11: 473–479.

10. Tønnesen P, Mikkelsen KL. Smoking cessation with four nicotine replacement regimes in a lung clinic. *Eur Respir J* 2000; 16: 717–722.

11. Tønnesen P. How to reduce smoking among teenagers. *Eur Respir J* 2002; 19: 1–3.

12. Martinet Y. Smoking Prevention Committee: promoting lung health through tobacco control. *ERS Newletter* May 2004; p. 3.

13. Paoletti P, Tønnesen P, Rodriguez-Rosin R. CEASE (Collaborative European Anti Smoking Evaluation): a challenging multicentre trail organized by the European Respiratory Society. *Eur Respir J* 1993; 6: 719–721.

14. Tønnesen P, Paoletti P, Gustavsson G, *et al.* Higher dosage nicotine patches increase one-year smoking cessation rates: results from the European CEASE trial. *Eur Respir J* 1999; 13: 238–246.

15. Pistelli F, Carrozzi L, Viegi G, Gulsvik A, Tønnesen P, the CEASE Collaborative Group. One year smoking abstinence promotes remission of respiratory symptoms: results from CEASE trial. *Eur Respir J* 2004; 24: Suppl. 48, 249s.

16. Palmiero G, Pistelli F, Aquilini F, *et al.* One year lung function variations in a multicenter European trial on smoking cessation (CEASE). *Eur Respir J* 2005; 26: Suppl. 49, 486s.

17. Monso E, Campbell J, Tønnesen P, Gustavsson G, Morera J. Socio-demographics predictors of success in smoking intervention. *Tob Control* 2001; 10: 165–169.

18. Carrozzi L, Pistelli F, Fornai E, Desideri M, Viegi G, Giuntini C. Smoking cessation clinic: an Italian experience. *Monaldi Arch Chest Dis* 2000; 55: 502–505.

19. Carrozzi L, Pistelli F, Viegi G. Pharmacotherapy for smoking cessation. *Ther Adv Respir Dis* 2008; 2: 301–317.

20. Lopes Pegna A, Picozzi G, Mascalchi M, *et al.* Design, recruitment and baseline results of the ITALUNG trial for lung cancer screening with low-dose CT. *Lung Cancer* 2008 Aug 22. [Epub ahead of print.]

21. Pistelli F, Aquilini F, Tavanti L, *et al.* Smoking cessation over the first year of follow-up in a lung cancer screening with spiral chest CT scan (Italung-CT study). *Eur Respir J* 2007; 30: Suppl. 51, 503s.

22. Loddenkemper R, Gibson GJ, Sibille Y, eds. Chronic obstructive pulmonary disease. *In*: European Lung White Book. The First Comprehensive Survey on Respiratory Health in Europe. Sheffield, European Respiratory Society Journals, 2003; pp. 34–43.

23. ASPECT Consortium. Tobacco or Health in the European Union: Past, Present and Future. Luxembourg, European Commission (Directorate-General for Health and Consumer Protection), 2004.

24. European Respiratory Society. Smoke Free Europe Conference 2005, jointly organised by ECL, EHN, ERS, French League against Cancer and Cancer Research UK, Luxembourg 2005. www.ers-education.org/pages/default.aspx?id=580 Date last accessed: 1 October 2008.

25. European Respiratory Society. ERS Research Seminar on Tobacco Smoking: Harm Reduction Strategies, Ferney-Voltaire 2005. www.ers-education.org/pages/default.aspx?id=578 Date last accessed: 1 October 2008.

26. Smoke Free Partnership. Lifting the Smokescreen: 10 Reasons for a Smoke Free Europe. Sheffield, European Respiratory Society Journals, 2006.
27. Tønnesen P, Carrozzi L, Fagerström KO, *et al.* Smoking cessation in patients with respiratory diseases: a high priority, integral component of therapy. *Eur Respir J* 2007; 29: 390–417.

CHAPTER 2

The role of chest physicians in tobacco control: a historical perspective. From health education in school to smoking cessation in hospitals

P. Bartsch

Correspondence: P. Bartsch, University of Liège, CHU Dept of Pneumology, Bd de l'Hôpital Bat. B35, Sart Tilman, 4000 Liège 1, Belgium. Fax: 32 43668846; E-mail: Pierre.Bartsch@ulg.ac.be

If history is examined for the first actions or statements about the fight against tobacco by doctors, it is not possible to find any chest physicians simply because specialised medicine did not exist at that time. In 1836, S. Green wrote the following: "[smoking] inflames the mouth and requires a perpetual flow of saliva, a fluid known to be among the most important to the whole economy of digestion; it irritates the eyes, corrupt the breath and causes thirst. No doubt the human frame may become so far accustomed to this drain, that the smoker may go on from year to year making himself a nuisance to society, yet there can be no doubt whatever, that the custom is deleterious in general as it is filthy" [1].

For centuries, tobacco was considered as a remedy *herbe propre à tous maux* [herb appropriate to every disease] until the isolation of nicotine and the demonstration of its poisonous qualities in 1828 [2].

During the nineteenth century, most doctors believed that moderate smoking in adults was not harmful, but that smoking was dangerous for children, this statement being inspired more by moral attitude than by any scientific evidence. Nevertheless, in 1908, the Children Act made it an offence to sell cigarettes to a juvenile aged <16 yrs [2].

The first documented link between illness and smoking amounting to more than a suspicion, during the 1940s and 1950s, was the issue of lung cancer [3]. Epidemiological studies were inspired by the fact that the cancer death rate was rising strikingly and continuously, from 4.9 per 100,000 population in 1930 to 75.6 per 100,000 population in 1990 [4].

Chest physicians and their associations had been involved, since the beginning of the twentieth century, in the fight against a major public health problem of that time, tuberculosis, which remains unresolved in the developing world. Nevertheless a shift to increasing attention for smoking health consequences was observed all over the world. In the American Lung Association, which was still called the National Association for the Study and Prevention of Tuberculosis, in 1956, increasing interest in asthma, chronic bronchitis, emphysema and other respiratory conditions occurred for the first time, as illustrated by the allocation of dedicated grants and fellowships.

In 1960, the board of directors of this association issued a warning about smoking as a policy statement: "Cigarette smoking is a major cause of lung cancer" [5].

The same progression was seen in tuberculosis associations in Europe and all over the world through the changes adopted at the International Union Against Tuberculosis,

Eur Respir Mon, 2008, 42, 8–16. Printed in UK - all rights reserved. Copyright ERS Journals Ltd 2008; European Respiratory Monograph; ISSN 1025-448x.

which became the International Union Against Tuberculosis and Lung Disease in 1986 following a proposal for an extension in mandate in 1973 [6].

If the role of chest physicians in the fight against tobacco was and remains important, it should be recognised that a determining factor in raising awareness about smoking and diseases was the work of epidemiologists, namely R. Doll and A.B. Hill, who made evident and indisputable the health effects of smoking [7].

More recently, the six leading world societies involved in lung diseases (American College of Chest Physicians, American Thoracic Society, Asian Pacific Society of Respirology, Canadian Thoracic Society, European Respiratory Society and International Union Against Tuberculosis and Lung Disease), the members of which are largely chest physicians, published a statement putting the issue of smoking and health as a physician's major responsibility [8]. In 2002, the American College of Chest Physicians published a position paper [9], issued along the lines of the practice guideline for tobacco cessation published in 1996 by the US Agency for Health Care Policy and Research [10], which was updated in 2000 [11].

In 2007, smoking cessation in patients with respiratory diseases was reported as a high priority component of therapy, by a task force on guidelines for smoking cessation appointed by the European Respiratory Society [12].

The conclusions of this expert panel are reported here because they set new standards for the profession of chest physicians in the present short historical review. "1) Patients with respiratory disease have a greater and more urgent need to stop smoking than the average smoker, so respiratory physicians must take a proactive and continuing role with all smokers in motivating them to stop and in providing treatment to aid smoking cessation. 2) Smoking cessation treatment should be integrated into the management of the patient's respiratory condition. 3) Therapies should include pharmacological treatment (*i.e.* nicotine replacement therapy, bupropion or varenicline) combined with behavioural support. 4) Respiratory physicians should receive training to ensure that they have the knowledge, attitudes and skills necessary to deliver these interventions or to refer to an appropriate specialist. 5) Although the cost of implementing these recommendations will partly be offset by a reduction in attendance for exacerbations, *etc.*, a budget should be established to enable implementation."

Health education in schools

In 1978, an international review regarding the effects of school programmes undertaken between 1960 and 1976 on smoking behaviour showed no effects on this outcome, despite several of the educational efforts demonstrating an improvement in the knowledge of the students benefiting from the anti-smoking programmes [13].

A prospective randomised controlled study was conducted in England and Wales, between 1988 and 1990, on 4,538 pupils allocated to two different education programmes, with a third group receiving both programmes and one group with no intervention serving as control group.

All four groups were evaluated before and immediately following teaching and 1 yr later, with 3,786 children remaining in the study. No significant differences were observed in smoking behaviour, health knowledge, beliefs or values between the four groups, but a significant increase in knowledge about smoking effects was seen [14].

An intervention aimed at preventing alcohol and tobacco abuse among 428 adolescents and 658 controls was carried out in a health unit in Lombardy (Italy) during 1989–1991. The conclusion was that the health education programme was unsuccessful in modifying behaviours and attitudes regarding alcohol and tobacco use during the 3-yr follow-up [15].

In 1994, the US Centers for Disease Control and Prevention (CDC) published "Guidelines for school health programs to prevent tobacco use and addiction" [16]. The guidelines recommend that all schools: 1) develop and enforce a school policy on tobacco use; 2) provide instruction about short- and long-term negative physiological and social consequences of tobacco use, social influences on tobacco use, peer norms regarding tobacco use and refusal skills; 3) provide tobacco-use prevention education from kindergarten to the twelfth grade; 4) provide programme-specific training for teachers; 5) involve parents or families in the support of school-based programmes to prevent tobacco use; 6) support cessation efforts among students and all school staff who use tobacco; and 7) assess the tobacco-use prevention programme at regular intervals. The guidelines deliver instructional concepts from early elementary school to senior high school divided into three different parts, knowledge, attitudes and skills.

An evaluation of the CDC guidelines in the state of Oregon (USA) published in 2001 [17] showed that this comprehensive school-based prevention programme, within a state-wide tobacco programme, may contribute to reductions in current smoking among eighth-grade students. Moreover, a greater decline in smoking prevalence was observed in schools in which the implementation of the programme was of higher level.

A cost-effectiveness study of a CDC-approved tobacco-use prevention programme, Towards No Tobacco Use, designed before the publication of the CDC guidelines, showed that, at an intervention cost of 16,403 US dollars (USD), Towards No Tobacco Use prevents 34.9 students from becoming established smokers. This corresponds to a saving of USD13,316 per life year saved and a saving of USD8,482 per quality-adjusted life year saved [18].

A Cochrane review published in 2002 [19] was more pessimistic since a summary of the conclusion is that "in half of the group of best quality studies, those in the intervention group smoke less than those in the control group, but many studies showed no effect of the intervention". An update of this review from 2006 [20] was not really more optimistic.

Regarding smoking cessation in youngsters aged <20 yrs, the Cochrane review [21] also reached a disappointing conclusion. "There were very few trials with evidence about pharmacological interventions (nicotine replacement and bupropion), and none demonstrated effectiveness for adolescent smokers.

"There is a need for well-designed adequately powered randomised trials for this population of smokers, with a minimum of six months follow up and rigorous definitions of cessation (sustained and biochemically verified)."

One message from the review is encouraging: "Complex approaches show promise, with some persistence of abstinence (30 days point prevalence abstinence at six months), especially those incorporating elements sensitive to stage of change."

Another programme meeting the CDC criteria, according to its authors [22], is now running in Colorado, USA (Tar Wars Program). It is supported by family physicians and claims effectiveness "in increasing students understanding about the short-term consequences of tobacco use, cost of tobacco use, truth of tobacco advertising, and peer norms". However, this article provides no data regarding the progression of smoking prevalence in the schools in which the intervention was conducted. In Belgium, a programme derived from Tar Wars, supported by the Belgian Society of Pneumology and benefiting from the free contribution of its members, has recently started and should be evaluated in the future.

A 2005 survey in the province of Luxembourg (Belgium), on 2,753 students aged 12–18 yrs, representing an 11.34% random sample of the total population (24,283 adolescents), revealed 22.6% smokers, 9.95% ex-smokers, 25.1% who had experimented with smoking and 42.3% never-smokers [23]. What is more interesting is that, among the 623 smokers, 42.7% would have liked to stop smoking, 36.5% were ambivalent and

20.8% did not want to stop. A very recent meeting organised by the regional Ministry of Health and the regional Ministry of Education (February 2007) confirmed that >40% of adolescent smokers are seeking help in smoking cessation. Thus, if prevention remains a challenge for physicians and educators together, the new and more difficult challenge of smoking cessation in adolescents is increasing.

Smoking cessation in hospitals

Smoking cessation in hospitalised patients has been promoted since the early 1990s, and slowly implemented with the help of activists working at the level of countries and Europe or on a worldwide basis. Even if there were some local initiatives, the European Commission, following the Empoli (Italy) resolution in 1994, created the European Network for Smoke-free Hospitals with France as a pilot. In the same year, the US joint commission on accreditation of healthcare organisations required that accredited hospitals be smoke-free [24].

In 1992, FAIRBANKS [25] expressed disappointment regarding the slow recognition of the value of smoke-free hospitals and the weakness of interest in the International Network Towards Smoke-free Hospitals.

There are very few articles regarding spontaneous smoking cessation rates following hospitalisation for an acute illness related to tobacco use. For example, the study of BAILE et al. [26] showed that 38% of patients hospitalised for acute myocardial infarction relapse during the in-hospital stay. Nevertheless the early relapse rate is related to less-severe myocardial infarction.

According to a French consensus conference, in the follow-up of an acute coronary disease, 25% of patients smoke after the acute event at 6 months, and 50% at 1 yr [27]. Some negative predictors for smoking cessation 12 months after a coronary event are a high level of nicotine addiction, a low level of self-confidence in quitting and having had previous coronary heart disease [28].

It is amazing that it is very difficult to find reports on spontaneous smoking cessation in chronic obstructive pulmonary disease (COPD) patients following hospitalisation for an exacerbation, and even studies on the effects of smoking cessation on the histopathological progression of the lungs are scarce and contradictory [29], despite the large consensus regarding the decrease in lung function impairment when smoking is abandoned.

The same group provided an insight into this issue in 2006, showing that, with longer duration of smoking cessation, COPD patients exhibit a decrease in CD8 cell and an increase in plasma cell counts in bronchial biopsy specimens [30].

Returning to the question of which COPD patients stop smoking, a very general analysis of Veterans Administration enrollees with COPD, a smoking history and aged >34 yrs (n=89,337) showed that those who have stopped smoking are older (69.6 versus 62.8 yrs), have more cardiac comorbid conditions, better mental health as shown by a psychological scoring questionnaire, participate more in their healthcare and have a better relationship with their provider than the active smokers [31]. The authors underlined the importance of taking into account underlying psychiatric comorbid conditions when addressing smoking cessation in COPD patients. No information is available regarding the possible interventions by the healthcare system in smoking cessation in the two groups, but the conclusions reported are coherent with other studies. This study did not target only hospitalised patients.

A randomised clinical trial on 74 smoking COPD patients compared simple advice to stop smoking in a nonsmoking unit to 15–20 min of counselling on alternate days while in hospital as regards smoking cessation rate at 3 and 6 months, with disappointing results [32].

In 1994, a survey conducted among the smokers who were hospitalised in a hospital with a nonsmoking policy about the amount of smoking cessation counselling received showed that 68% received one out of nine counselling procedures, 48% more than one and only 15% information about nicotine withdrawal symptoms and care. None of the patients had smoking cessation included in plans for the future [33].

A randomised study on >2,000 patients hospitalised in four hospitals demonstrated that a multicomponent smoking cessation programme was superior to less-intensive interventions. Smoking cessation rates in this group were 27% at 1 yr compared with 22% with the less-intensive intervention and 20% in the usual-care group [34].

The ineffectiveness of low-intensity interventions was confirmed by another study on 650 smokers who were given a short intervention programme or usual care. At 6 months, there was no difference between the intervention group and the controls. Nevertheless the authors reported a difference in the result of the programme on smokers that had never previously tried to quit smoking (15.3 *versus* 3.7%) [35].

A Cochrane review published in 2001 concluded that "High intensity behavioural interventions that include at least one month of follow-up contact are effective in promoting smoking cessation in hospitalised patients. The findings of the review were compatible with research in other settings showing that NRT increases quit rate" [36]. The 2003 review arrived at exactly the same conclusions.

This conclusion was confirmed by a study that compared two groups of patients who benefited from two different programmes of smoking cessation starting when hospitalised, combining transdermal nicotine replacement therapy (NRT) with behavioural intervention. The two groups differed only in the intensity of psychological support: the first received minimal intervention and the second intensive counselling plus telephone follow-up as outpatients [37]. There was a 35% quit rate in the intensive group compared with 21% in the first group at 6 months; at 1 yr, the rates were 33 compared to 20%. The patients came from a coronary disease unit.

A more recent prospective cohort study in Australia [38] was conducted in a cardiothoracic hospital setting. The programme was based on individual counselling on behavioural modification, including written information, advice about quit aids and support during the quit attempt. After 12 months, the point prevalence abstinence rate, controlled by exhaled carbon monoxide measurement, was 32%. This result was obtained despite the fact that 25% of the initial cohort, lost to follow-up, were considered to be continuing smokers.

Chest physicians could perhaps use spirometry as an aid to smoking cessation, as suggested by some reports [39–41]. The impact of spirometry seems measurable whether behavioural support is mild [39] or intensive [40]. The repetition of spirometry when airflow limitation is present increases smoking cessation annually [41]. The strategy of systematic spirometric screening, as a public health measure, could help smoking cessation in the general population, as suggested by BEDNAREK *et al.* [42], even without pharmacotherapy. Of course, as indicated by systematic reviews, NRT should increase the quit rate.

In specific hospitalisation settings, such as psychiatric hospitals, some short-term results as regards abstinence can be obtained by the combination of NRT, motivational interviewing and cognitive behaviour therapy. In the longer term, a clear reduction in daily cigarette consumption was obtained even when selection was made for psychotic disease [43].

The integration of smoking cessation intervention within psychiatric care was recommended for patients with post-traumatic stress disorder in two articles by the same

Seattle research team [44, 45]. The same integration of smoking cessation intervention for in-patients treated for substance abuse was recommended some years ago [46].

Nevertheless, when the intervention is limited to NRT in a smoke-free psychiatric hospital, all patients observed returned to smoking within 5 weeks of discharge from hospital. Thus the authors concluded that greater support was needed within the hospital and following discharge in order to maintain abstinence [47].

In the present short review, other situations, such as smoking cessation in adolescents with psychiatric disorders [48] or hospitalised in an emergency department [49], have not been considered, smoking cessation in adolescents at large being particularly difficult.

Other situations of great interest, such as smoking cessation in cancer patients or perioperative smoking cessation, are also not be covered in the present chapter.

Conclusion

The role of chest physicians in the history of tobacco control is difficult to track because the history of the fight against tobacco is very long, even if a start is not made from James I and *A Counterblaste to Tobacco* [50], published in 1604! Moreover, as stated previously, when the medical profession began to be aware of the threat of smoking to health, specialised medicine did not exist.

Nevertheless chest physicians were among the first to become sensitised to the illnesses attributable mostly to smoking and they shifted from the white plague of tuberculosis to the world epidemics of tobacco. Their associations were very active in promoting the idea that caring about smoking issues was an important task for the profession, and, more recently, the involvement of chest physicians in smoking cessation was strongly recommended [12].

Concerning school programmes, it is difficult to identify the chest physicians among the promoters of such actions, but, at least in Belgium, the role of the profession and its association in promoting and delivering the programme in schools is known. The present authors urge their colleagues to identify themselves as actors in the tobacco field, the best way being participation in group 06.03 of the European Respiratory Society! Indeed, some of their activities remain unpublished.

The same remarks can apply to the activity of chest physicians in the hospitals in which they work, even if the activity of some of them, such as B. Dautzenberg in the European Network for Smoke-free Hospitals, is known.

Chest physicians very often play the leading role in hospitals, in running smoking cessation clinics. They are aware that they are increasingly followed by cardiologists, accompanied by psychiatric departments, and encouraged by the anaesthesiology sector and public health servants. This general medical mobilisation is, of course, needed, as the importance and difficulty of the task and the necessity of a multidisciplinary approach, together with an intense lobbying activity aimed at politicians, is known.

It is also mandatory to show the scientific community that tobacco dependence and its treatment represent a truly fascinating scientific issue.

Summary

The history of the evolving opinion of physicians regarding tobacco is briefly reviewed here.

The position of chest physicians has been influenced more by the progressive expansion of specialised medicine than by a specific gift of chest physicians. Nevertheless, their professional associations, which dealt with a large public health challenge, namely tuberculosis, were prepared to be rapidly sensitised by the new challenge, again concerning mainly the lungs, represented by the tobacco smoking epidemics.

The ERS itself urges chest physicians to be part of challenging the disease represented by nicotine dependence, by means of both a training including expertise in smoking cessation and being in close relationship with behaviour specialists if they do not want to improve their skills in that specific area.

As regards what happens in schools, it is quite difficult to identify the chest physicians among the promoters of health education scenarios concerning smoking, but it can be stated that the Belgian Society of Pneumology officially encourages its members to use a slide kit developed by a chest physician in the schools in the vicinity of their practices.

If what is happening in hospitals regarding smoking cessation during or before hospital stay is considered, it is clear that lung or heart and lung departments are most active in this field. Again chest physicians can be identified among the promoters in their own country, but most of these activities are not published or appear only in the grey literature.

Keywords: Chest physicians, health education in schools, smoking cessation, tobacco history.

References

1. Green S. Smoking. *In*: New England Almanack and Farmers' Friend. New London, Starr & Co., 1836; pp. 25–26.
2. Walker RB. Medical aspects of tobacco smoking and the anti-tobacco movement in Britain in the nineteenth century. *Med Hist* 1980; 24: 391–402.
3. Wynder EL, Graham EA. Tobacco smoking as a possible etiological factor in bronchogenic carcinoma: a study of 684 proven cases. *JAMA* 1950; 143: 329–336.
4. American Cancer Society. Cancer Facts and Figures 1999. Atlanta, American Cancer Society, 1999.
5. American Lung Association. History. www.lungusa.org/site/c.dvLUK9O0E/b.23686/k.DE87/history.htm Date last updated: 2008.
6. International Union Against Tuberculosis and Lung Disease. History of the Union. www.theunion.org/about-the-union/history-of-the-union.html Date last updated: 2008. Date last accessed: 1 December 2008.
7. Doll R, Hill AB. The mortality of doctors in relation to their smoking habits: a preliminary report. *BMJ* 1954; ii: 2451–2455.
8. American College of Chest Physicians, American Thoracic Society, Asia Pacific Society of Respirology, Canadian Thoracic Society, European Respiratory Society, International Union

Against Tuberculosis and Lung Disease. Smoking and health: a physician's responsibility. A statement of the joint committee on smoking and health. *Eur Respir J* 1995; 8: 1808–1811.

9. Anderson JE, Jorenby DE, Scott WJ, Fiore MC. Treating tobacco use and dependence: an evidence based clinical practice guideline for tobacco cessation. *Chest* 2002; 121: 932–941.

10. Agency for Health Care Policy and Research. Smoking cessation clinical practice guideline. *JAMA* 1996; 275: 1270–1280.

11. The Tobacco Use and Dependence Clinical Practice Guideline Panel, Staff, and Consortium Representatives. A clinical practice guideline for treating tobacco use and dependence: a US Public Health Service Report. *JAMA* 2000; 283: 3244–3254.

12. Tonnesen P, Carrozzi L, Fagerström KO, *et al.* Smoking cessation in patients with respiratory diseases: a high priority, integral component of therapy. *Eur Respir J* 2007; 29: 390–417.

13. Thompson EL. Smoking education programs 1960–1976. *Am J Public Health* 1978; 68: 250–257.

14. Nutbeam D, Macaskill P, Smith C, Simpson JM, Catford J. Evaluation of two school smoking education programmes under normal classroom conditions. *BMJ* 1993; 306: 102–107.

15. Donato F, Monarca S, Coppini C, *et al.* Evaluation of a health education program for preventing alcohol and tobacco use in a health unit in Lombardy, Italy. *Epidemiol Prev* 1996; 20: 24–30.

16. Anon. Guidelines for school health programs to prevent tobacco use and addiction. *MMWR Recomm Rep* 1994; 43: 1–18.

17. Centers for Disease Control and Prevention. Effectiveness of school-based programs as a component of a state wide tobacco control initiative – Oregon, 1999–2000. *MMWR Morb Mortal Wkly Rep* 2001; 50: 663–666.

18. Wang LY, Crossett L, Lowry R, Sussman S, Dent CW. Cost-effectiveness of a school-based tobacco use prevention program. *Arch Pediatr Adolesc Med* 2001; 155: 1043–1050.

19. Thomas R. School-based programmes for preventing smoking. *Cochrane Database Syst Rev* 2002; Issue 4: CD 001293.

20. Thomas R, Perera R. School-based programmes for preventing smoking. *Cochrane Database Syst Rev* 2006; Issue 3: CD 001293.

21. Grimshaw GM, Stanton A. Tobacco cessation intervention for young people. *Cochrane Database Syst Rev* 2006; Issue 4: CD 003289.

22. Cain DJ, Dickinson WP, Fernald D, Bublitz C, Dickinson LM, West D. Family physicians and youth tobacco-free education: outcomes of the Colorado Tar Wars Program. *J Am Board Fam Med* 2006; 19: 579–589.

23. Demelenne M. Prévalence du tabagisme chez les adolescents issus de l'enseignement secondaire de la Province du Luxembourg-2005. [Prevalence of smoking among secondary school adolescents in the province of Luxemburg 2005.] www.fares.be

24. Mc Kee M, Gilmore A, Novotny TE. Smoke free hospitals. An achievable objective bringing benefits for patients and staff. *BMJ* 2003; 326: 941–942.

25. Fairbanks LL. International Network Towards Smoke-free Hospitals. *Tob Control* 1992; 1: 59.

26. Baile WF Jr, Bigelow GE, Gottlieb SH, Stitzer ML, Sacktor JD. Rapid resumption of cigarette smoking following myocardial infarction: inverse relation to MI severity. *Addict Behav* 1982; 7: 373–380.

27. French Agency for Health Accreditation and Evaluation. Conférence de consensus. Arrêt de la consommation du tabac. [Consensus Conference. Stop Using Tobacco.] www.tabac-info-service.fr/data/pdf/conference-ANAES.pdf Date last updated: October 1998. Date last accessed: 1 December 2008.

28. Quist-Paulsen P, Bakke PS, Gallefoss F. Predictors of smoking cessation in patients admitted for acute coronary heart disease. *Eur J Cardiovasc Prev Rehabil* 2005; 12: 472–477.

29. Willemse BW, Postma DS, Timens W, ten Hacken NH. The impact of smoking cessation on respiratory symptoms, lung function, airway responsiveness and inflammation. *Eur Respir J* 2004; 23: 464–476.

30. Lapperre TS, Postma DS, Gosman MM, Lee S, Anzueto A. Relation between duration of smoking cessation and bronchial inflammation in COPD. *Thorax* 2006; 61: 115–121.

31. Adams SG, Pugh JA, Kazis LE, *et al.* Characteristics associated with sustained abstinence from smoking among patients with COPD. *Am J Med* 2006; 119: 441–447.

32. Pederson LL, Wanklin JM, Lefcoe NM. The effects of counseling on smoking cessation among patients hospitalized with chronic obstructive pulmonary disease: a randomized clinical trial. *Int J Addict* 1991; 26: 107–119.

33. Neighbor WE Jr, Stoop DH, Elsworth A. Smoking cessation counseling among hospitalized smokers. *Am J Prev Med* 1994; 10: 140–144.

34. Miller NH, Smith PM, De Busk RF, *et al.* Smoking cessation in hospitalized patients. Results of a randomized trial. *Arch Intern Med* 1997; 157: 409–415.

35. Rigotti NA, Arnsten JH, McKool KM, Wood-Reid KM, Pasternak RE, Singer DE. Efficacy of smoking cessation program for hospital patients. *Arch Intern Med* 1997; 157: 2653–2660.

36. Rigotti NA, Munafo MR, Murphy MF, Stead LF. Interventions for smoking cessation in hospitalized patients. *Cochrane Database Syst Rev* 2001; Issue 2: CD 001837.

37. Simon JA, Carmody TP, Hudes ES, *et al.* Intensive smoking cessation counseling *versus* minimal counseling among hospitalized patients treated with transdermal nicotine replacement: a randomized trial. *Am J Med* 2003; 114: 555–562.

38. Fung PR, Snape-Jenkinson SL, Godfrey MT, *et al.* Effectiveness of hospital-based smoking cessation. *Chest* 2005; 128: 216–223.

39. Gorecka D, Bednarek M, Nowinski A, Puscinska E, Goljan-Geremek A, Zielinski J. Diagnosis of airflow limitation combined with smoking cessation advice increases stop-smoking rate. *Chest* 2003; 123: 1916–1923.

40. Kennedy DT, Paulson DM, Eddy TD, *et al.* A smoking cessation program consisting of extensive counseling, pharmacotherapy, and office spirometry: results of a pilot project in Veterans Administration Medical Center. *Pharmacotherapy* 2004; 24: 1400–1407.

41. Stratelis G, Mölstad J, Jakobsson P, Zetterström O. The impact of repeated spirometry and smoking cessation advice in smokers with mild COPD. *Scand J Prim Health Care* 2006; 24: 133–139.

42. Bednarek M, Gorecka D, Wielgomas J, *et al.* Smokers with airway obstruction are more likely to quit smoking. *Thorax* 2006; 61: 869–873.

43. Baker A, Richmond R, Haile M, *et al.* A randomized controlled trial of smoking cessation intervention among people with a psychotic disorder. *Am J Psychiatry* 2006; 163: 1934–1942.

44. McFall M, Saxon AJ, Thompson CE, *et al.* Improving the rates of quitting smoking for veterans with posttraumatic stress disorder. *Am J Psychiatry* 2005; 162: 1311–1319.

45. McFall M, Atkins DC, Yoshimoto D, *et al.* Integrating tobacco cessation treatment into mental health care for patients with posttraumatic stress disorder. *Am J Addict* 2006; 15: 336–344.

46. Joseph AM, Nichol KL, Willenbring ML, Korn JE, Lysaght LS. Beneficial effects of the treatment of nicotine dependence during an inpatient substance abuse treatment program. *JAMA* 1990; 263: 3043–3046.

47. Prochaska JJ, Fletcher L, Hall SE, Hall SM. Return to smoking following a smoke-free psychiatric hospitalization. *Am J Addict* 2006; 15: 15–22.

48. Brown RA, Ramsey SE, Strong DR, *et al.* Effects of motivational interviewing on smoking cessation in adolescents with psychiatric disorders. *Tob Control* 2003; 12: Suppl. 4, IV3–IV10.

49. Horn K, Dino G, Hamilton C, Noerachmanto N. Efficacy of an emergency department-based motivational teenage smoking intervention. *Prev Chronic Dis* 2007; 4: A08.

50. James I. A Counterblaste to Tobacco. London, R. Barker, 1904.

CHAPTER 3

Smoking cessation in public health and in clinical practice: two different perspectives for the chest physician

S. Nardini

Correspondence: S. Nardini, Pulmonary and TB Unit, General Hospital, ULSS 7, Via Forlanini, 71, 31029 Vittorio Veneto, Treviso, Italy. E-mail: snardini@qubisoft.it

In Western countries, the interventions that can reduce the impact of tobacco smoking (especially smoking cessation) and, consequently, smoking-related health damage are the most effective interventions in community medicine when effectiveness and cost-effectiveness are taken into consideration [1, 2].

Since most respiratory diseases are caused by smoking, chest physicians should know both the essentials of tobacco control and the interventions for smoking cessation.

As for tobacco control in general, a bundle of interventions are available (table 1), comprised mainly of social, regulatory and market interventions, which can reduce the appeal and availability of tobacco products. The prevention of smoking initiation among youngsters is one of these interventions; treatment of smokers for cessation (*i.e.* management of nicotine addiction) is also included in this list.

Smoking cessation can be delivered at either the primary care level or the specialist level, with differing and increasing intensity. Ideally, each respiratory medicine unit should include a smoking cessation service, similar to what is already carried out in tuberculosis management, where respiratory units treat the patients with the disease and manage contacts and persons at risk of developing tuberculosis. Generally speaking, such a clinic, while operating at the clinical level by delivering diagnosis and (intensive) treatment of its own patients and being a reference for the general practitioner and other primary care professionals (the so-called second level of intervention), also acts at the community level by helping in the planning of primary care interventions and preventive actions, training health professionals and lobbying policy makers.

The prevention of initiation and assistance in cessation are not two mutually exclusive strategies. Rather, they can support each other since the prevention of initiation gives results after decades, whereas cessation after weeks or months. Besides, it has been suggested that youngsters are perhaps best helped to avoid initiation if the prevalence of smoking among adults is systematically driven down [4].

In smoking cessation there are also two levels of intervention, the first one on healthy smokers, to prevent a smoking-related disease, and the second on smokers suffering from a disease caused by smoking.

The present chapter deals with the generalities of tobacco control and smoking cessation from the point of view of the respiratory physician.

Prevention of initiation

Eight out of ten smokers start smoking during adolescence, a period of life when the personality is not completely developed and health messages are useless, and a person

Eur Respir Mon, 2008, 42, 17–22. Printed in UK - all rights reserved. Copyright ERS Journals Ltd 2008; European Respiratory Monograph; ISSN 1025-448x.

Table 1. – Tobacco control standard: recommendations of the Surgeon General (2000)

Educational strategies
Management of nicotine addiction
Regulatory efforts
   Advertising and promotion
   Product regulation
   Clean indoor air regulation
   Minors' access to tobacco
   Litigation approaches
Economic approaches
Comprehensive programmes
Global efforts
Elimination of health disparities

Data taken from [3].

who smokes during adolescence has 16 times the risk of becoming an adult smoker [5]. Practically all youngsters experience smoking; their eventual take-up of the habit depends upon both social and genetic factors. The former explain the exposure to first cigarettes, whereas the latter form the basis of continued smoking and development of addiction.

Some tens of cigarettes are sufficient to permanently modify the structure and function of nicotine receptors in the brain, thus determining addiction [6], and addiction is the most powerful obstacle to quitting.

The key step, according to this evidence, is that prevention of smoking initiation should be the best way of fighting tobacco-related harm. This idea is both attractive and simple in conception; if quitting smoking is so difficult, then the best and easiest thing to do is not to start [7]. However, as appealing as this idea is, the reality is much less promising; the prevalence of smoking among youngsters remains high notwithstanding strong efforts to fight it, and the marked reduction in smoking prevalence in industrialised countries observed during recent decades has occurred due more to quitting among smokers than to reduced initiation.

The reasons behind this trend are that, against the aggressive marketing of the tobacco companies, the actions of governmental and nongovernmental organisations has been discontinuous, fragmented and not part of a comprehensive strategy fighting for tobacco control.

Generally speaking, smoking initiation can be coped with by using interventions that reduce offer (*i.e.* accessibility of tobacco products) or reduce demand (*i.e.* motivation among youngsters to take up the habit).

Offer can be regulated with laws and bans, and demand can be reduced by heath education (*e.g.* in schools) and mass media campaigns.

Demand can be stimulated through advertising, since the youth form a strategic market for tobacco companies [8]. This advertising is both direct and (especially where banned, as in Italy) indirect, with sponsorship of sports or cultural events or leisure garments.

The offer is conditioned by laws and bans, availability of vending machines, and heavier or lighter taxation.

In recent years, both school- and community-based programmes have tried to reduce initiation to tobacco smoking. School-based curricula proved to be completely ineffective, unless coupled to mass media campaigns, smoking bans and community-based programmes. However, even when interventions coupled these activities, the evidence was not particularly strong [9]. Family-based interventions seem to be promising, but there are very few good quality trials to be conclusive [10].

Since, if individuals are not smokers before the age of 20 yrs, there is only a low probability that they will become smokers as adults, there is a case for programmes for young people including not only prevention but also treatment (*i.e.* smoking cessation) [11]. However, so far, the experience of assisted quitting among young smokers had been understudied and no conclusions can be drawn [12].

In conclusion, to date, most studies fail to support the use of interventions to prevent the uptake of smoking among young people (unless part of comprehensive approaches), whereas more attention should be devoted to smoking cessation in this age group.

Smoking cessation

Unlike prevention of smoking initiation, smoking cessation does not lack evidence. On the contrary, there is overwhelming and convincing evidences that this kind of intervention is effective and cost-effective. Moreover, chest physicians are told by almost all recent guidelines that smoking cessation is the first and most effective treatment of respiratory patients [13]. Even in patients suffering from surgically untreatable lung cancer, smoking cessation can increase life expectancy and quality of life. Thus smoking cessation should form part of everyday routine in chest medicine. Unfortunately, this is not the case.

Indeed, there are some differences regarding how smoking cessation is delivered, depending upon which kind of patient (and in what kind of situation) is to be treated (table 2). In other words, there is a difference between helping a 30-yr-old male who starts the attempt to quit because his new girlfriend is a nonsmoker and helping a 55-yr-old male suffering from a chronic respiratory disease that has caused him to be hospitalised due to respiratory failure. This is analogous to the way in which hypertension control has a different priority in an otherwise healthy individual than in a person who has undergone a myocardial infarction.

These examples make it clear that, in smoking cessation, at least two levels of intervention can be identified, which, referring to different patient populations, can be classified into the following two different perspectives.

1) The public health perspective. This is when smoking cessation is intended as a general intervention in a general population; the smoker who desires to attempt to quit starts the attempt alone (in most cases) or seeking assistance (rarely). In this case, the focus is on the advantage to the community. Smoking cessation is the most important intervention that can be carried out to improve the health of the community; a half of smokers are killed by their habit and a quarter are killed aged 35–69 yrs. Smoking cessation reduces harm and damage; the sooner the smoker quits the better. Quitting before the age of 30 yrs makes the risk of death the same as in never-smokers. The results of this first level of intervention come from the great number of smokers potentially involved in the intervention. Even if smoking cessation, from a public health perspective, is not very effective (as it is the case of minimal advice, bringing a 3–5% cessation excess *versus* no intervention), the overall result is good because a great number of people quit.

Table 2. – Levels of smoking cessation intervention

Intervention level	Smoker	Intervention type	Health staff involved
First	Healthy smoker	Minimal	Primary care
Second	Unhealthy smoker	Intensive	Specialist

2) The clinical perspective. This is when smoking cessation is intended as part of the treatment of a patient suffering from (or at great risk of) a smoking-related disease. In this case, the advantage is to the individual, and arises from the probability that they will succeed in remaining abstinent in the long term. Only a very effective treatment can give good results in this case. As in every clinical situation, a great number of resources are concentrated at the same time and in the same individual in order to maximise the possible effect.

Thus, in the first case, it is better to use resources that are widespread and cost-effective, even if poorly effective, because the aim is to deliver the most diffuse treatment; even nonmedical strategies can be used (price policies, regulations, bans, *etc.*). The target is obviously the young and healthy population, since, in this case, the gain to public health is the greatest.

In the second case, all resources, the more effective the better, have to be used because the aim is to deliver the most effective treatment, even if, in this case, the gain to public health is low (as in many clinical situations) because the target is the older and/or ill population (table 2).

This distinction should be clearly made because it emphasises why and in what sense the treatment for smoking cessation of a respiratory (or cardiological or neoplastic) patient is different from the usual smoking cessation approach.

A problem that arises from this line of reasoning is the issue of motivation [14, 15], which is dealt with extensively in another chapter of the present Monograph.

From the public health perspective, motivation can be (and, indeed, is considered) the essential starting point. As the probability that an attempt starts depends upon motivation, treatment should be offered only to motivated people. According to guidelines, if the patient is not motivated, attempts should be made to elicit motivation (see following paragraph). If unsuccessful, the physician (or, generally speaking, health professional) repeats the advice on the following contact. In other words, the physician should delay the therapy.

This approach does not seem acceptable in smoker respiratory (or cardiac or cancer) patients. Although smoking cessation is universally considered the first-line therapy in most respiratory diseases, respiratory patients are more dependent upon tobacco and have tried quitting many times, with frequent relapses and becoming somehow waterproof to smoking cessation advice. Thus some of them continue smoking even when receiving long-term oxygen therapy [16, 17]. This situation can lead the physician to believe that a smoking cessation intervention is impossible.

On the contrary, intervention in smoker respiratory patients should be considered in a completely different way to the same intervention in healthy smokers (see chapter on motivation).

Unfortunately, there are very few studies on smoking cessation in this population of patients, and no study at all on unmotivated ones.

The other difficulty is that smoking cessation has not been (and is not) part of the education and training courses in medical schools, meaning that any physicians has either to learn to practise it, or to refer the patient to health facilities or organisations that can deliver the treatment.

A flow chart can be proposed for the management of smokers (fig. 1). The professional in charge of smoker management (the subject of the flow chart) is the general practitioner, but the steps can be the same for every chest physician.

If the patient is a smoker, they should be asked about their willingness to try quitting in a very short time. If they want to try, then the physician (or health professional) should assist the patient according to the standard. If they do not want to try, then the physician should weigh the priority of the smoking cessation attempt. If quitting is a priority, as in patients with a respiratory condition (*e.g.* chronic obstructive pulmonary

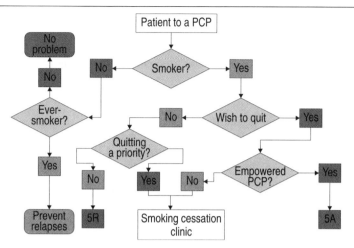

Fig. 1. – Flow chart for managing smokers for smoking cessation. PCP: primary care professional. Reproduced with permission from [18].

disease, lung cancer or asthma), then an intensive treatment should be delivered, either in the smoking cessation clinic or directly in the chest unit by a smoking cessation specialist.

Conclusions

Smoking cessation (*i.e.* the management of nicotine addiction) forms part of a comprehensive approach to tobacco control, which includes regulatory, educational and economic interventions.

Smoking cessation has different meanings in preventive and in clinical settings; in the former, it prevents diseases, and, in the latter, it treats established diseases.

In as far as it is recognised that smoking cessation is the first and most important intervention in the management of respiratory patients, the existence of these two populations, healthy and ill smokers, should be acknowledged because they differ in the meaning of their habit and in their priority for treatment (the latter should be treated for quitting as soon as possible).

Based on these differences in perspective, assistance should differ such that the smoker respiratory patient is always proposed an intensive treatment in a dedicated setting (*e.g.* the smoking cessation clinic).

References

1. Jha P, Chaloupka FJ, eds. Curbing the epidemic. Governments and the Economics of Tobacco Control. Washington, DC, World Bank, 1999..
2. Parrott S, Godfrey C. Economics of smoking cessation. *BMJ* 2004; 328: 947–949.
3. US Department of Health and Human Services. Reducing Tobacco Use. A Report of the Surgeon General. Atlanta, US Department of Health and Human Services, Centers for Disease Control and Prevention, National Center for Chronic Disease Prevention and Health Promotion, Office on Smoking and Health, 2000.

4.   Jamrozik K. ABC of smoking cessation. Policy priorities for tobacco control. *BMJ* 2004; 328: 1007–1009.

5.   Chassin L, Presson CC, Sherman SJ, Edwards DA. The natural history of cigarette smoking: predicting young-adult smoking outcomes from adolescent smoking patterns. *Health Psychol* 1990; 9: 701–716.

6.   US Department of Health and Human Services. The Health Consequences of smoking. Nicotine Addiction. A report of the Surgeon General. Atlanta, Center for Health Promotion and Education, Office on Smoking and Health, 1988.

7.   US Department of Health and Human Services. Preventing Tobacco use among Young People. A Report of the Surgeon General. Atlanta, US Department of Health and Human Services, Public Health Service, Centers for Disease Control and Prevention, National Center for Chronic Disease Prevention and Health Promotion, Office on Smoking and Health, 1994.

8.   Sepe E, Ling PM, Glantz SA. Smooth moves: bar and nightclub tobacco promotions that target young adults. *Am J Public Health* 2002; 92: 414–419.

9.   Thomas R, Perera R. School-based programmes for preventing smoking. *Cochrane Database Syst Rev* 2006; Issue 3: CD001293.

10. Thomas RE, Baker P, Lorenzetti D. Family-based programmes for preventing smoking by children and adolescents. *Cochrane Database Syst Rev* 2007; Issue 1: CD004493.

11. Mermelstein R. Teen smoking cessation. *Tob Control* 2003; 12: Suppl. 1, i25–i34.

12. Grimshaw GM, Stanton A. Tobacco cessation interventions for young people. *Cochrane Database Syst Rev* 2006; Issue 4: CD003289.

13. Tønnesen P, Carrozzi L, Fagerström KO, *et al.* Smoking cessation in patients with respiratory diseases: a high priority, integral component of therapy. *Eur Respir J* 2007; 29: 390–417.

14. Prochaska JO, Di Clemente CC. Towards a comprehensive model of change. *In*: Miller WR., Heather N., eds. Treating Additive Behaviours: Processes of Change. New York, Plenum Press, 1986; pp. 3–27.

15. Prochaska JO, Velicer WF, Prochaska JM, Johnson JL. Size, consistency, and stability of stage effects for smoking cessation. *Addict Behav* 2004; 29: 207–213.

16. Restrick LJ, Paul EA, Braid GM, Cullinan P, Moore-Gillon J, Wedzicha JA. Assessment and follow up of patients prescribed long term oxygen treatment. *Thorax* 1993; 48: 708–713.

17. Morrison D, Skwarski K, MacNee W. Review of the prescription of domiciliary long term oxygen therapy in Scotland. *Thorax* 1995; 50: 1103–1105.

18. Nardini S, Vianello S, Barbano G, Cagnin R. La disassuefazione dal fumo nel Veneto: un modello di intervento. *Aria Ambiente e Salute* 2005; 3: 8–12.

CHAPTER 4

The costs of smoking and the economics of smoking cessation

C. Lazzaro*, S. Nardini#

*Health economics office, Milan, and #Pulmonary and TB Unit, General Hospital, Vittorio Veneto, Italy.

Correspondence: C. Lazzaro, Health economics office, Via Stefanardo da Vimercate, 19, I-20128 Milan, Italy. Fax: 39 226000516; E-mail: carlo.lazzaro@tin.it

Smoking-related mortality and morbidity are matters of paramount interest for healthcare policy-makers. The US Center for Disease Control and Prevention estimates that smoking kills ~419,000 people annually in the USA, and should be held responsible for a third of all deaths among working-age Americans [1].

According to a recent survey carried out in 11 European countries, among a sample of 407,541 males aged 45–59 yrs, 8.3% of deaths (ranging from 4.2% in Portugal to 11.9% in Switzerland) were attributable to lung cancer [2]. Other lung diseases (International Classification of Diseases 460–519) were held responsible for 4.5% of deaths in Europe (ranging from 2.9% in Norway to 7.2% in Ireland) and 3.3% in Italy [1]. Although there is no clear evidence that smoking in itself is the cause of these deaths, the authors emphasised that cigarette addiction may increase mortality risk for all types of pulmonary disease [2].

Smoking reduces life expectancy at birth in both males (69.7 *versus* 77.0 yrs for nonsmokers) and females (75.6 *versus* 81.6 yrs for nonsmokers) [3].

According to another survey, the smoking prevalence in Italy is 31.5% among males (16 cigarettes·day^{-1}, on average) and 17.2% among females (12 cigarettes·day^{-1}, on average) [4]. Although it has been ascertained that smoking is responsible for 90% of lung cancer, 66% of chronic obstructive pulmonary disease (COPD) [5] and 25% of cardiovascular diseases, and leads to 84,000 deaths·yr^{-1} [4], ~41,400 Italians take up smoking annually [6].

Considering the high debt of avoidable diseases and premature deaths paid to tobacco addiction, the following paragraphs focus on the following topics: the costs of smoking-related diseases, the cost-effectiveness of lung cancer screening, and, particularly, the economics of smoking cessation.

Costs of smoking-related diseases

Although both epidemiological and clinical data concerning smoking-related diseases are widely available, less is known regarding the costs of smoking-related diseases borne by the healthcare sector, patients and their families, and society as a whole.

A US study reported the difference in medical expenditure for people with smoking-related diseases compared to those without to be 6 billion US dollars (USD) [7]. In the Netherlands, when inflated to 1997 prices, the lifetime cost of smoking-related diseases was estimated at USD7.27 billion for males and USD9.47 billion for females [8]. It is

Eur Respir Mon, 2008, 42, 23–34. Printed in UK - all rights reserved. Copyright ERS Journals Ltd 2008; European Respiratory Monograph; ISSN 1025-448x.

noteworthy that the above-mentioned figures do not include the societal costs associated with premature death or the loss of working days due to smoking-related morbidity.

A cost of illness study carried out in Germany [9] estimated total smoking-related healthcare costs to be 5.47 billion Euros (EUR; 73% of the overall disease-related costs) for COPD, EUR2.59 billion (89%) for lung cancer, EUR1 billion (65%) for cancer of the mouth and larynx, EUR1.77 billion (28%) for stroke, EUR4.96 billion (35%) for coronary artery disease and EUR0.76 billion (28%) for atherosclerotic occlusive disease. The economic burden of smoking-related healthcare costs for Germany is EUR16.6 billion, with smoking being responsible for 47% of the total costs of these diseases, *i.e.* EUR35.2 billion.

The annual costs to the UK National Health Service (NHS) of adult smoking-related disease approach EUR2.3 billion [10, 11]. UK costs related to premature deaths due to smoking are estimated at EUR130 billion; lung cancer is associated with 5.7% of all smoking-related NHS costs. Of these healthcare costs, 90% of lung cancer costs result from hospital rather than primary care [11].

The healthcare-related costs due to smoking for Italy were calculated as a contribution to the development of the international deterministic population-based model, Economic Consequences of Smoking (ECOS), endorsed by the World Health Organization (WHO) in line with the 1999 Action Plan for a Tobacco-Free Europe. The ECOS model estimates the health and economic burden of smoking-related diseases across all of the European Union countries and Australia, Canada, China, Czech Republic, Hungary, Mexico, New Zealand, Norway, Poland and Ukraine. The first version of the model was presented on May 31, 1999, on World No-Tobacco Day. The model is in the public domain and can be accessed *via* a dedicated European WHO Website [6].

The global burden of healthcare-related cost of smoking for Italy was estimated at EUR4.31 billion (cardiovascular diseases 2.46, COPD 0.45, small cell lung cancer 0.06, nonsmall cell lung cancer 0.23, and stroke 1.11); all amounts are expressed at 1998 values [12].

When non-healthcare-related costs are considered, losses from fires caused by smoking materials are estimated at ~0.004 billion UK pounds (GBP) per annum in Scotland [13] and GBP0.15 billion per annum in England and Wales [11].

As far as costs related to loss of productivity are concerned, a recent Scottish survey showed absenteeism to be higher among smokers compared to nonsmokers [13]. The estimated cost of smoking-related absence in Scotland is GBP0.04 billion per annum [13], whereas total productivity losses are estimated at ~GBP0.45 billion per annum [11].

Lung cancer screening: is it good value for money?

Is lung cancer screening cost-effective?

Since smoking is one of the most acknowledged risk factors for lung cancer [4, 14, 15], health economists and physicians dealing with the clinical and economic consequences of respiratory diseases are frequently asked whether or not early detection of lung cancer is cost-effective. However, what does the term cost-effective really mean?

Cost-effectiveness analysis and the meaning of cost-effective

Cost-effectiveness analysis (CEA) is a model of full economic evaluation of healthcare programmes comparing both the costs and consequences of two or more alternatives aimed at a single common effect on a patient's survival and/or health state [16].

In CEA, outcomes are measured in non-monetary units (*e.g.* number of deaths avoided and number of years of life saved) [16], and these outcomes are then related to the costs incurred *via* incremental analysis [16, 17].

Incremental analysis simply divides the difference in costs (incremental cost) by the difference in effectiveness (incremental effectiveness) of the compared healthcare programmes [16, 17]. The result of CEA is the incremental cost-effectiveness ratio (ICER; *e.g.* the cost per incremental year of life saved). This ratio quantifies the costs that need to be borne by a healthcare provider in order to obtain an additional unit of relevant clinical outcome with respect to a comparator(s). Hence the ICER means the cost to be borne by a given stakeholder for obtaining an incremental unit of effectiveness from a given healthcare programme (*e.g.* the cost for obtaining an additional year of life with an antihypertensive drug that is more costly and more effective than a programme for early detection of lung cancer).

Some authors claim that CEA results can also be expressed in terms of incremental cost per incremental quality-adjusted life year (QALY) gained [17].

An effective healthcare programme should be considered cost-effective whenever its costs are justified on the grounds of the effect on a patient's health state when compared, *via* incremental analysis, to the best available alternative [18].

As far as the cost per year of life (or per QALY) saved is concerned, a threshold of USD50,000 is usually considered the general rule for accepting healthcare programmes that are both effective and cost-effective (*i.e.* with an ICER falling within USD50,000 per year of life or per QALY gained) and disregarding healthcare programmes that are effective but not cost-effective (*i.e.* with an ICER of >USD50,000 per year of life or per QALY gained) [19].

Cost-effectiveness of lung cancer screening

There is a strong case for justifying early detection of lung cancer on economic grounds [20], as the costs and consequences of lung cancer screening are partially related to an improvement in long-term mortality. However, according to the results of three main US trials comparing lung cancer screening *versus* not screening [21–23], long-term mortality does not seem to differ between the two arms of the studies [24].

The costs related to screening are not only those of the early detection procedure but also those related to: 1) setting up a screening programme, 2) enrolling patients, 3) following-up patients with positive results at the time of screening, and 4) checking-up those patients with false positive results at the time of screening.

Possible future savings in the cost of detection and treatment must be compared with the cost of lung cancer screening, *i.e.* the cost related to the screening procedure itself together with all of the other kinds of costs mentioned above.

There is a tight relationship between time and the accrual of the cost and consequences of screening or not screening on a patient's health state. According to time preference theory [16, 17, 25], people prefer to face a cash outlay tomorrow rather than today, and, consistently, to improve their health state today rather than tomorrow [16, 17, 25]. Hence future costs and consequences should be converted into their present value *via* discounting. Indeed, discounting makes the costs and consequences accrued with different timing comparable. Currently, the accepted real (*i.e.* regardless of inflation) discount rate for costs and, in general [26], consequences is 3% [16, 17].

Since early detection of lung cancer entails a stream of costs and consequences "starting now and stretching away into the future" [20], whereas the costs and consequences related to no screening programme become evident in the future, screening for lung cancer is likely not to be cost-effective compared to not screening due to discounting.

Despite proposals for increasing the cost-effectiveness of lung cancer screening [27], especially for high-risk patients with a long-term smoking addiction [28], there is strong evidence that current computed tomography (CT)-supported programmes aimed at the early detection of lung cancer are, in general, not cost-effective.

The base-case estimated cost of lung cancer screening with helical CT, ranging USD116,300–2,300,000 per QALY gained [29, 30], is probably unaffordable for a huge number of healthcare systems. Besides, both bounds of the range are well over the threshold of USD50,000 per year of life (or per QALY) saved [19]. Only considering the most favourable estimates for all of the relevant economic hypotheses included in the above-mentioned CEA, a programme screening current smokers is USD42,500 per QALY gained [29].

In a recent Italian trial on early detection of lung cancer with spiral CT and positron emission tomography in long-term heavy smokers [31], the cost-effectiveness issue was not addressed. However, the authors claimed that lung cancer screening programmes were unlikely to reach an interesting cost–benefit balance compared to other medical priorities [31].

Owing to the high cost per incremental QALY gained with lung cancer screening, fighting smoking addiction remains the only rational measure for preventing lung cancer [24].

Economics of smoking cessation

Cost-effectiveness of smoking cessation interventions

As far as the economics of smoking cessation are concerned, all interventions aimed at stopping smoking are highly cost-effective compared to other healthcare programmes.

According to one of the most famous examples of a league table, which are, basically, directories of healthcare programmes ranked from the lowest to the highest cost per year of life [32], or, more often, per QALY gained [16, 17, 33], with a cost per QALY of GBP270 in 1990 prices, giving up smoking following a general practitioner's (GP's) advice was considered good value for money and ranked third in a list of 21 medical and surgical interventions aimed at preventing or treating different diseases [33].

Among healthcare programmes aimed at COPD patients, when expressed in 1990–1991 prices, the cost per year of life gained following smoking cessation therapy was USD6,500 [32], whereas the cost per year of life gained following a pulmonary rehabilitation programme or α_1-antitrypsin deficit therapy approached USD24,300 or USD50,000, respectively [34].

When expressed in 1997 prices, smoking cessation interventions were more cost-effective (USD2,700 per year of life saved) than other healthcare programmes targeted to different diseases, such as mammographic screening (USD50,000 per year of life saved) and treatment of high cholesterol level (USD100,000 per year of life saved) [35, 36].

One of the most important contributions to the cost-effectiveness of smoking cessation interventions carried out in the UK had a reported cost per year of life saved ranging from EUR354 (GP's brief advice to stop smoking) to EUR1,458 (GP's advice plus self-help plus advice to purchase nicotine replacement therapy (NRT) with specialist services) when inflated to 1998 prices. All of these figures included healthcare as well as non-healthcare related cost [10, 11].

According to a UK cost-effectiveness model comparing different smoking cessation interventions from the UK NHS viewpoint, the incremental cost per year of life saved is ~GBP1,000–2,399 for NRT, ~GBP639–1,492 for bupropion sustained release (SR) and ~GBP890–1,969 for NRT plus bupropion SR [37].

As part of a set of guidelines on smoking cessation for Italian GPs, a CEA was performed for the comparison of two hypothetical interventions aimed at smoking cessation in a GP setting [15]. The selected alternatives were primary care (*i.e.* a GP's advice about quitting smoking) and cessation clinic (*i.e.* a GP's advice plus NRT). When inflated to 2000 prices, the healthcare-related costs were EUR87.18 and 266.89 for primary care and cessation clinic, respectively. On the grounds of previous evidence [38], the effectiveness of primary care and cessation clinic considered in the model were 7 and 17%, respectively. When compared to the option of doing nothing, the ICER was EUR1,245.43 for primary care and EUR1,797.10 for cessation clinic, respectively.

Which of these programmes is implemented in the real world depends upon the share of the Health Authority (HA) budget allocated to smoking cessation policies and interventions.

At first glance, the above-mentioned percentages of quitters might be considered low. However, as reported in a recent UK study, it seems noteworthy that, at a cost of GBP100 per 1% increase in 6-month continuous abstinence rate, the cost per year of life gained for 40-yr-old smokers would be ~GBP6,600 [39].

The Italian findings seem to be consistent with those reported in a Danish study aimed at assessing the real-life data-based cost-effectiveness of smoking cessation interventions *versus* no intervention in various subgroups of smokers; the ICER was estimated at EUR1,358 per incremental quitter [40].

A Markov chain model that simulated two cohorts of smokers (a reference cohort given brief cessation counselling by a GP; and a treatment cohort given counselling plus pharmacotherapy, including nicotine gum, patch, spray and inhaler, and bupropion) in six Western countries (Canada, France, Spain, Switzerland, the USA and the UK) was also interesting [41]. The cost per year of life saved by counselling alone ranged from USD190 in Spain to USD773 in the UK for males, and from USD288 in Spain to USD1,168 in the UK for females. The incremental cost per year of life saved for gum ranged from USD2,230 for males in Spain to USD7,643 for females in the USA; for patch ranged from USD1,758 for males in Spain to USD5,131 for females in the UK; for spray ranged from USD1,935 for males in Spain to USD7,969 for females in the USA; for inhaler ranged from USD3,480 for males in Switzerland to USD8,700 for females in France; and for bupropion ranged from USD792 for males in Canada to USD2,922 for females in the USA.

In all of the above-mentioned research, whenever years of life saved were considered, the related ICER fell well below the USD50,000 ceiling [19].

Quality-adjusted life years and the economics of smoking cessation: handle with care

Despite the fact that CEA usually places interventions aimed at smoking cessation near the top of league tables, this result should be interpreted with a lot of caution [10], since a low cost per incremental QALY gained does not tell the whole story

According to a part of the literature dealing with priority setting in healthcare, QALYs can be interpreted according to two different theories [42]. The first theory claims that, since resources are limited, the most efficient means of maximising the health state of a given society is to produce as many low cost per QALY programmes as possible. Besides, being QALYs-production-neutral with respect to the user of healthcare programmes (*i.e.* giving each year of life the same weight regardless of who benefits from it), also increases equity within society.

This latter statement is harshly criticised by proponents of the second, opposing, theory, which states that, far from ensuring equity, QALYs favour the better off on the following grounds. 1) A set of non-strictly-related healthcare conditions (*e.g.* living in healthy environment, pursuing a good level of education and being aware that smoking is harmful) benefits wealthier people and makes them more likely to exhibit a lower cost per QALY gained compared to poorer people. As far as smoking cessation policies are concerned, this remark is of paramount importance, since better-off patients are probably less prone to developing smoking addiction in the long run and more compliant with interventions aimed at stopping smoking than worse-off people. According to an extensive inquiry into inequalities in health carried out in the UK [43, 44], the greatest reductions in smoking prevalence occurred in the better off, whereas the worse off reported comparatively little benefit [45]. 2) In general, the QALYs criterion may disadvantage the elderly, disabled persons (especially for life-threatening diseases) and severely ill patients.

Beyond the league tables: other factors affecting the effectiveness of smoking cessation interventions

Smoking cessation and schooling. Research carried out in the USA attempted to identify some relationships between duration of schooling and the percentage of smokers who gave up after an educational programme [46]. The best result (-40%) was obtained among smokers who reported >15 yrs of schooling; this was followed by smokers with 13–15 yrs of schooling (-24%) and those with <12 yrs of schooling (-7%). Again, the best result, obtained among people with the greatest school attendance, may probably be explained by the consideration that they came from better-off families.

Smoking cessation and cigarette taxation. Following a 10% increase in cigarette taxation, a poor 4% reduction in smoking among all smokers and a more-interesting 14% reduction among smoking teenagers were reported for the USA [44]. As explained in the following paragraph (as regards price elasticity), this probably occurred because teenagers are highly price-sensitive smokers, since they can rely on a lower disposable income than adult working smokers. As 90% of smokers take up tobacco consumption during their teenage years, higher cigarette taxation may reduce smoking addiction, especially in the long run [47, 48].

Smoking cessation and price elasticity of current cigarette smokers. Price elasticity (*i.e.* the expected reduction in cigarette consumption following an increase in cigarette price) is inversely related to a smoker's age. Empirical research on this topic in the USA reported the lowest price elasticity (-0.095) among smokers aged 27–29 yrs and the highest (-0.831) among those aged 15–17 yrs [49].

The theory of rational addiction may explain these results [50–52]. This theory claims that smoking addiction, like a stock of capital, increases with time. Thus the longer the smoking addiction the lower the probability that the smoker will give up owing to an increase in cigarette price.

Again, the relevant role of cigarette price in preventing transition from experimental smoking (teenagers) to more regular smoking (adults) [47, 48] should be conveniently taken into account by healthcare policy-makers, since, quoting the above-mentioned results [49], a 1% increase in cigarette price may result in an 83.1% reduction in cigarette consumption among teenagers.

Smoking cessation and job. According to the results of a broad epidemiological survey including 12 European countries [2], the mortality rate for lung cancer in male manual workers aged 45–49 yrs ranges from 1.07 (Portugal) to 2.20 (Finland) times higher than that reported for non-manual workers. Since manual workers often belong to poorly educated clusters of the population, they may be unaware of all of the damages related to tobacco addiction and thus less determined to quit smoking than more educated smokers. These patients may benefit from workplace-delivered smoking cessation interventions [53]. Workplace-delivered healthcare programmes have been successfully implemented for the management of other diseases (*e.g.* hypertension) [54].

Role of general-practitioner-led interventions in smoking cessation strategies

Recent UK research performed on a sample of London-based GPs highlighted the fact that the GPs' perceptions about the effectiveness of smoking cessation services influence their intentions to recommend these services [55]. The importance of correctly addressing GPs' beliefs on smoking cessation programmes has been addressed by a Swiss research group [56]; the cost-effectiveness of adequately training GPs in smoking cessation counselling *versus* currently accepted tobacco control interventions reached USD25.4 per incremental year of life saved for males and USD35.2 for females [56].

As far as GP-led smoking cessation interventions are concerned, the Italian experience may be of some interest. Italian GPs are paid a capitation fee of ~EUR30 for each patient signed up [57]. This amount funds the whole GP activity, including healthcare educational programmes and smoking cessation counselling. As cigarette addiction is one of the most alarming public health issues, some HAs agree with their GPs on a monetary benefit to be paid for each patient who gives up smoking following GP-led intervention. The amount of the monetary benefit is ~EUR500, and the GP is given EUR350 as soon as the former smoker self-declares on a HA form that they have quit cigarettes following GP-led intervention. The physician is given the remaining part of the monetary benefit 2 yrs later, provided that the former smoker is confirmed as a nonsmoker following a set of tests (carboxyhaemoglobin, spirometry and research into nicotine urinary catabolites) performed for the district HA [58, 59].

The cost of drugs prescribed by the GP for supporting smoking cessation intervention is currently borne entirely by the patient. However, a recent Dutch study has pointed out that reimbursement for smoking cessation drugs may be cost-effective if society is willing to pay EUR10,000 for an additional quitter or EUR18,000 for an incremental QALY gained [60].

Conclusion

Four concluding remarks seem to be worth making concerning the present chapter on the costs of smoking and the economics of smoking cessation.

1) As far as lung cancer screening is concerned, the long-term costs and consequences for a patient's health state that may accrue from screening programmes or not screening should be carefully considered [20]. Focusing attention on the economic side of this issue, the above-mentioned research supports the evidence that, even when effective, CT-supported programmes aimed at the early detection of lung cancer are probably not good value for money because they are not cost-effective compared to not screening. Hence there is one more good reason for replacing secondary prevention of lung cancer screening with primary prevention (*i.e.* not taking up smoking).

2) Based on wide differences in price elasticity [49] and according to the theory of rational addiction [50–52], high cigarette taxation and prices play a relevant role in

reducing future smoking addiction among teenagers [47,48], but not among long-term adult smokers.

3) Interventions aimed at smoking cessation show a low cost per QALY (or per year of life) gained. However, a favourable ICER is probably not the only relevant criterion to be considered when policies and strategies targeted at smoking cessation have to be implemented. In order to increase the effectiveness of programmes aimed at stopping smoking, information on the clusters of the population that seem to have major problems with cigarette consumption compared to the rest of society should be collected. A UK cross-sectional study performed on a cohort of subjects as part of the European Prospective Investigation into Cancer (EPIC-Norfolk) [61] underlined the importance of this issue by investigating whether social class, educational level and residential deprivation level were independently related to cigarette smoking habit in both males and females. The authors reported the multivariate age-adjusted odds ratios (ORs) for current smoking in males to be 1.62 (95% confidence interval (CI) 1.45–1.81) for manual compared to non-manual social class, 1.32 (95% CI 1.17–1.48) for those with less than zero educational level compared to those with zero level qualification or higher, and 1.84 (95% CI 1.62–2.08) for high *versus* low area deprivational level. When the same analysis was performed in females, the ORs for current smoking were 1.14 (95% CI 1.03–1.27) for manual social class, 1.31 (95% CI 1.18–1.46) for low educational level and 1.68 (95% CI 1.49–1.90) for high residential deprivation level.

Enrolling worse-off people, low-schooling persons and manual workers who are addicted to tobacco in *ad hoc* smoking cessation programmes (*e.g.* workplace-delivered tobacco dissuasion sessions) may initially increase the cost per QALY of these interventions but will probably reduce the global prevalence of smokers in the future to a greater extent.

4) Among the currently available smoking cessation interventions, a GP's or specialist's advice plus NRT plus bupropion SR seems to represent good value for money [35]. Based on its low ICER, reported in various international research [62, 63], NRT has been prescribed in primary care in the UK since April 2001 [11].

Summary

The economic burden of smoking-related diseases, such as cardiovascular disease, chronic obstructive pulmonary disease, stroke and lung cancer, borne by healthcare systems and society as a whole is relevant.

Even when effective healthcare programmes aimed at the early detection of lung cancer in long-term heavy smokers are not cost effective compared to not screening, since the cost per quality-adjusted life year gained may reach >2,300,000 US dollars (USD), well over the threshold of USD50,000 reported in the literature. This poor result can be explained by the consideration that costs and consequences related to not screening become evident in the future and should be valued less highly than those accruing at the time of screening.

All interventions aimed at stopping smoking are highly cost-effective compared to other healthcare programmes. In the UK, the cost per year of life saved following smoking cessation interventions ranged from 354 Euros (EUR; general practitioner's brief advice to stop smoking) to EUR1,458 (general practitioner's advice plus self-help plus advice to purchase nicotine replacement therapy with specialist services) when inflated to 1998 prices.

However, a favourable incremental cost-effectiveness ratio is probably not the only relevant criterion to be considered whenever policies and strategies targeted at smoking cessation have to be implemented. Information on the clusters of the population that seem to have major problems with cigarette consumption compared to the rest of society (worse-off people, low-schooling persons and manual workers) should be taken into account, since they are usually poorly compliant with smoking cessation therapies. Enrolling such patients into *ad hoc* smoking cessation programmes may initially increase the cost per year of life (or per quality-adjusted life year) saved by these interventions, but will probably reduce the global prevalence of smokers in the future to a greater extent.

Keywords: Cost-effectiveness, lung cancer screening, smoking cessation.

References

1. Nair AK, Brandt EN Jr. Effects of smoking on health care costs. *J Okla State Med Assoc* 2000; 93: 245–250.
2. Kunst AE, Groenhof F, Mackenbach JP, on behalf of the EU Working Group on Socioeconomic Inequalities in Health. Occupational class and cause specific mortality in middle aged men in 11 countries: comparison of population based studies. *BMJ* 1998; 316: 1636–1642.
3. Doll R, Peto R, Wheatley K, Gray R, Sutherland I. Mortality in relation to smoking: 50 years' observations on male British doctors. *BMJ* 1994; 309: 901–911.
4. Decreto del Presidente della Repubblica 23 Maggio 2003. Approvazione del Piano sanitario nazionale 2003–2005. [President of the Republic Decree 23 May 2003. Passage of the National Health Plan 2003–2005.] Gazzetta Ufficiale [Official Gazette of the Italian Republic] ordinary supplement. General series No. 139. 18 June 2003. Rome, Istituto Poligrafico e Zecca dello Stato [Italian Mint], 2003.
5. Ministry of Health, Decreto del Presidente della Repubblica 23 Luglio 1998. Piano sanitario nazionale 1998–2000. Un patto di solidarietà per la salute. [President of the Republic Decree 23

July 1998. National Health Plan 1998–2000. A solidarity-based agreement for health.] Rome, Istituto Poligrafico e Zecca dello Stato [Italian Mint], 1998.

6. World Health Organization, Economic Consequences of Smoking (ECOS) model. WHO European Partnership Project to Reduce Tobacco Dependence. www.who.dk/adt/ecos/whoweb.asp Date last updated: 31 May 1999. Date last accessed: 15 January 2004.

7. Johnson E, Dominici F, Griswold M, Zeger SL. Disease cases and their medical costs attributable to smoking: an analysis of the national medical expenditure survey. *J Econom* 2003; 112: 135–151.

8. Barendregt JJ, Bonneux L, van der Maas J. The health care costs of smoking. *New Engl J Med* 1997; 337: 1052–1057.

9. Ruff LK, Volmer T, Nowak D, Meyer A. The economic impact of smoking in Germany. *Eur Respir J* 2000; 16: 385–390.

10. Parrott S, Godfrey C, Raw M, West R, McNeill A. Guidance for commissioners on the cost effectiveness of smoking cessation interventions. *Thorax* 1998; 53: Suppl. 5, S1–S38.

11. Godfrey C. The economic and social costs of lung cancer and the economics of smoking prevention. *Monaldi Arch Chest Dis* 2001; 56: 458–461.

12. Health and Economic Consequences of Smoking (ECOS) Model. WHO European Partnership Project to Reduce Tobacco Dependence. Appendix 1. www.who.dk/adt/ecos/WHOManual/app.htm#appitaly Date last updated: 31 May 1999. Date last accessed: 15 January 2004.

13. Parrott S, Godfrey C, Raw M. Costs of employee smoking in the workplace in Scotland. *Tob Control* 2000; 9: 187–192.

14. Woloshin S, Schwartz LM, Weick HG. Tobacco money: up in smoke? *Lancet* 2002; 358: 2108–2111.

15. Invernizzi G, Nardini S, Bettoncelli G, *et al.* L'intervento del Medico di Medicina Generale nel controllo del fumo. [The general practitioner's intervention in controlling smoking addiction.] *Rass Patol App Respir* 2002; 17: 55–70.

16. Drummond MF, Schulper MJ, Torrance GW, O'Brien BJ, Stoddart GL. Methods for the Economic Evaluation of Health Care Programmes. 3rd Edn. Oxford, Oxford University Press, 2005.

17. Gold MR, Siegel JE, Russel LB, Weinstein MC. Cost-Effectiveness in Health and Medicine. New York, Oxford University Press, 1996.

18. Doubilet P, Weinstein MC, McNeil B. Use and misuse of the term "cost-effective" in medicine. *N Engl J Med* 1985; 5: 293–309.

19. Mark DB, Hlatky MA, Califf RM, *et al.* Cost effectiveness of thrombolytic therapy with tissue plasminogen activator as compared with streptokinase for acute myocardial infarction. *N Engl J Med* 1995; 332: 1418–1424.

20. Cairns J. The costs of prevention. *BMJ* 1995; 311: 1520.

21. Melamed M, Flehinger B, Zamam M, Heelan R, Perchick W, Martini N. Screening for early lung cancer. Results of the Memorial Sloan Kettering study in New York. *Chest* 1984; 86: 44–53.

22. Fontana RS. Early detection of lung cancer: the Mayo project. *In*: Prorock PC., Miller AB., eds. Screening for Cancer. Geneva, International Union Against Cancer, 1984, pp. 107–122.

23. Tockman MS, Levin ML, Frost JK, Ball WC, Stitik FP, Marsh BR. Screening and detection of lung cancer. *In*: Aisner J., ed. Lung Cancer. New York, Churchill Livingstone, 1985; pp. 25–36.

24. Ciatto S. Screening oncologici. [Cancer screening.] In: Ciatto S., ed. Screening in Medicina. [Screening in Medicine.] Rome, Il Pensiero Scientifico Editore, 1996; pp. 127–157.

25. Hodgson TA, Meiners MR. Cost-of-illness methodology: a guide to current practices and procedures. *Millbank Mem Fund Q Health Soc* 1982; 60: 429–462.

26. van Hout BA. Discounting costs and effects: a reconsideration. *Health Econ* 1998; 7: 581–594.

27. Miettinen OS. Screening for lung cancer: can it be cost-effective? *Can Med Assoc J* 2000; 162: 1431–1436.

28. Henschke CI, McCauley DI, Yankelevitz DF, *et al.* Early Lung Cancer Action Project: overall design and findings from baseline screening. *Lancet* 1999; 354: 99–105.

29. Mahadevia PJ, Fleisher LA, Frick KD, Eng J, Goodman SN, Powe NR. Lung cancer screening with helical computed tomography in older adult smokers: a decision and cost-effectiveness analysis. *JAMA* 2003; 289: 313–322.

30. Swensen SJ. Screening for cancer with computed tomography. *BMJ* 2003; 326: 894–895.

31. Pastorino U, Bellomi M, Bandoni C, *et al.* Early lung-cancer detection with spiral CT and positron emission tomography in heavy smokers: 2-year results. *Lancet* 2003; 362: 593–597.

32. Schulmann KA, Lorna AL, Glick HA, Eisenberg J. Cost effectiveness of low-dose zidovudine therapy for asymptomatic patients with human immunodeficiency virus (HIV) infection. *Ann Intern Med* 1991; 114: 798–802.

33. Maynard A. Developing the health care market. *Econ J* 1991; 101: 1277–1286.

34. Rutten-Van Mölken MPMH, Van Doorslaer EKA, Rutten FFH. Economic appraisal of asthma and COPD care: a literature review 1980–1981. *Soc Sci Med* 1992; 35: 161–175.

35. Cromwell J, Bartosch WJ, Fiore MC, Hasselblad V, Baker T. Cost-effectiveness of the clinical practice recommendations in the AHCPR guideline for smoking cessation. Agency for Health Care Policy and Research. *JAMA* 1997; 278: 1759–1766.

36. Fiore MC, Bailey WC, Cohen SJ, *et al.*, Treating Tobacco Use and Dependence. Clinical Practice Guideline. Agency for Healthcare Research and Quality Publication No. 00-0032. Rockville, US Department of Health and Human Services, Public Health Services; 2000; p. 111.

37. NHS Centre for Reviews & Dissemination, A Rapid and Systematic Review of the Clinical and Cost Effectiveness of Bupropion SR and Nicotine Replacement Therapy (NRT) for Smoking Cessation. York, NHS Centre for Reviews & Dissemination University of York, 2002.

38. Nardini S. Percorsi terapeutici nella abitudine al fumo. [Therapeutic pathways in smoking addiction.] Proceedings of the Milan Health Congress 1999. Workshop No. 11: Standardizzazione degli interventi più frequenti in medicina generale. [Standardisation of the most frequent healthcare procedures in general medicine.] Milan, MOSAN, 1999.

39. West R. The clinical significance of "small" effects of smoking cessation treatments. *Addiction* 2007; 102: 506–509.

40. Olsen KR, Bilde L, Juhl HH, *et al.* Cost-effectiveness of the Danish smoking cessation interventions: subgroup analysis based on the Danish Smoking Cessation Database. *Eur J Health Econ* 2006; 7: 255–264.

41. Cornuz J, Gilbert A, Pinget C, *et al.* Cost-effectiveness of pharmacotherapies for nicotine dependence in primary care settings: a multinational comparison. *Tob Control* 2006; 15: 152–159.

42. Rationing in the NHS. Principles and Pragmatism. London, King's Fund, 1996; pp. 58–59.

43. Department of Health, Independent Inquiry into Inequalities in Health. London, Stationery Office, 1998.

44. Acheson D, Baker D, Illsley R. Inequalities in Health. *BMJ* 1998; 317: 1659.

45. Whitfield L. Social policies "must focus on inequalities". *Health Serv J* 1998; 108: 8.

46. Terris M. Healthy lifestyles. The perspective of epidemiology. *J Public Health Policy* 1992; 13: 186–193.

47. Tobacco Taxation. www.impacteen.org/generalarea_PDFs/NCSLSEATTLE111601.pdf Date last updated: 10 December 2001. Date last accessed: 20 January 2004.

48. Price, Tobacco Control Policies and Youth and Young Adult Tobacco Use. www.impacteen.org/generalarea_PDFs/TUPTI084201 Date last updated: 10 December 2001. Date last accessed: 20 January 2004.

49. Harris JE, Chan SW. The continuum-of-addiction: cigarette smoking in relation to price among Americans aged 15–29. *Health Econ* 1999; 8: 81–86.

50. Becker GS, Murphy KM. A theory of rational addiction. *J Polit Econ* 1988; 96: 675–700.

51. Becker GS, Grossman M, Murphy KM. An empirical analysis of cigarette addiction. *Am Econ Rev* 1994; 84: 396–418.

52. Chaloupka FJ, Tauras J, Grossman M. Economic Models of Addiction and Applications to Cigarette Smoking and other Substance Abuse. Chicago, University of Illinois, 1999; pp. 1–27.

53. Abbritti G, Muzi G, Latini L, *et al.* Health promotion in the occupational setting: what are the prospects in the Italian situation? *Med Lav* 2000; 91: 515–530.

54. Logan A, Milne B, Achber C, Campbell W, Haynes R. Cost-effectiveness of a worksite hypertension program. *Hypertension* 1981; 3: 211–218.

55. Vogt F, Hall S, Marteau TM. General practitioners' beliefs about effectiveness and intentions to recommend smoking cessation services: qualitative and quantitative studies. *BMC Fam Pract* 2007; 8: 39–49.

56. Pinget C, Martin E, Wasserfallen JB, Humair JP, Cornuz J. Cost-effectiveness analysis of a European primary-care physician training in smoking cessation counseling. *Eur J Cardiovasc Prev Rehabil* 2007; 14: 451–455.

57. Donatini A, Rico A, D'Ambrosio MG, *et al.* Financial resource allocation. *In*: Rico A, Cetani T, eds. The Healthcare Systems in Transition (HiT). Italy. Copenhagen, European Observatory on Health Care Systems, 2001; pp. 83–90.

58. Donzelli A, Perozziello F. Progetto aziendale per la disassuefazione dal fumo degli assistiti dei medici di medicina generale. [A Health Authority project for smoking cessation in GPs' patients.] *Agenzia Sanitaria Italiana* 2001; 3: 36–40.

59. Donzelli A, Perozziello F. Alcune domande e risposte sul progetto aziendale di disassuefazione dal fumo da parte dei MMG. [Questions and replies about the GP-led Health Authority project for smoking cessation.] Agenzia Sanitaria Italiana, 2001; 3: 41–45.

60. Kaper J, Wagena EJ, van Schayck CP, Severens JL. Encouraging smokers to quit: the cost effectiveness of reimbursing the costs of smoking cessation treatment. *Pharmacoeconomics* 2006; 24: 453–464.

61. Shohaimi S, Luben R, Wareham N, *et al.* Residential area deprivation predicts smoking habit independently of individual educational level and occupational social class. A cross sectional study in the Norfolk cohort of the European Investigation into Cancer (EPIC-Norfolk). *J Epidemiol Community Health* 2003; 57: 270–276.

62. Stapleton J, Lowin A, Russell M. Prescription of transdermal nicotine patches for smoking cessation in general practice: evaluation of cost-effectiveness. *Lancet* 1999; 354: 210–215.

63. Bolin K, Lindgren B, Willers S. The cost utility of bupropion in smoking cessation health programs: simulation model results for Sweden. *Chest* 2006; 129: 651–660.

CHAPTER 5

Review of current smoking cessation guidelines

C. Gratziou

Correspondence: C. Gratziou, Smoking Cessation Clinic, Pulmonary and Critical Care Dept, Evgenidio Hospital, Medical School, Athens University, 20 Papadiamantopoulou Street, 11528 Athens, Greece. Fax: 00 30 2107272785; E-mail: Cgratziou@med.uoa.gr

The problem of nicotine addiction

Nicotine addiction is a chronic relapsing condition that can be difficult to treat. There are ~1.1 billion people worldwide who use tobacco products, and most of these want to stop [1]. Of smokers, ~70% report that they want to quit, a third of them try to stop smoking each year, but only 20% of them seek help [2–4]. Most quit attempts are unassisted (will-power alone) and are associated with low success rates (3–5%) [5]. In addition, the majority of people who successfully stop smoking relapse. Smokers have a higher rate of success when they seek help with quitting. Even then, giving up permanently is difficult and several attempts are often required before long-term abstinence is achieved [2–4].

Smoking cessation and prevention strategies have tremendous potential for improving public health. For instance, the risk of coronary heart disease has been estimated to decrease by 50% 12 months after smoking cessation [5]. The relative risk of developing other conditions, such as chronic obstructive pulmonary disease (COPD), lung cancer and stroke, also decreases with smoking cessation [2, 6, 7]. Stopping smoking reduces the accelerated decline in pulmonary function and improves long-term prognosis [7]. Thus, as recommended by the Global Initiative for Chronic Obstructive Lung Disease, smoking cessation is the most important therapeutic intervention in the management of COPD [8].

Old and current guidelines

Given that the health benefits of stopping smoking are enormous, and that significant morbidity, mortality and economic effects are attributed to smoking, clinical practice guidelines have been published that provide recommendations for interventions and strategies for promoting the treatment of tobacco dependence. A number of such smoking cessation guidelines have been published in recent years.

In the USA, the Agency for Health Care Policy and Research (AHCPR) published clinical practice guidelines for treating tobacco use and dependence in 1996 [9]. These were the first comprehensive evidence-based guidelines for the clinical treatment of tobacco addiction, and represented a review of >3,000 articles on tobacco addiction published during 1975–1994. These guidelines were designed to provide clinicians with specific information regarding effective treatment for smoking cessation. The American College of Chest Physicians (ACCP) participated in the implementation of the original guideline recommendations.

Eur Respir Mon, 2008, 42, 35–43. Printed in UK - all rights reserved. Copyright ERS Journals Ltd 2008; European Respiratory Monograph; ISSN 1025-448x.

An updated version of these guidelines was released in 2000 by the US Public Health Service [10] and published in *JAMA* in 2000 as "A clinical practice guideline for treating tobacco use and dependence" [11], and was focused on primary care clinicians, tobacco dependence treatment specialists and healthcare administrators. These new guidelines were based primarily on meta-analyses of a total of 6,000 articles and randomised clinical trials, and were peer-reviewed and commented upon by 70 external reviewers. The updated guidelines addressed the treatment of tobacco use in special populations, such as pregnant females, hospitalised smokers, children and adolescents, and older smokers. Based on these guidelines, an ACCP position paper entitled "Treating tobacco use and dependence: an evidence-based clinical practice guideline for tobacco cessation" [12] was published in *Chest* in 2002 in order to highlight the key strategies and recommendations to chest clinicians for delivering effective interventions for tobacco cessation that fulfil the mandate for high-quality patient care.

Practical guidelines with a focus on smokers for whom primary care treatment has failed, psychiatric patients and patients in smoke-free facilities were reported by the American Psychiatric Association (APA), also in 1996 [13]. The recommendations within this report are based on evaluations of randomised controlled trials and clinical experience and are similar to those of the AHCPR. These guidelines are intended primarily for psychiatrists; however, they may be useful to all clinicians caring for nicotine-dependent patients.

In 1998, the UK Health Education Authority commissioned the development of smoking cessation guidelines for health professionals in the UK [14]. The recommendations within these guidelines were based upon systematic reviews of the Cochrane Collaboration Tobacco Addiction Review Group and AHCPR and APA guidelines. These guidelines were updated in 2000 [15], and outline ways in which to treat tobacco dependence and reduce the burden of death and illness associated with tobacco use.

In 1998, the UK government released a White Paper on tobacco, outlining proposals to help motivated smokers to quit [16]. In April 2002, the National Institute for Clinical Excellence in the UK released a document providing guidance to healthcare professionals on the use of pharmacotherapy with nicotine replacement therapy (NRT) and bupropion hydrochloride for smoking cessation [17]. Guidelines have also been developed and published by the National Health Committee in New Zealand [18] and the Canadian Task force on Preventive Health Care [19].

Internationally, World Health Organization recommendations propose core interventions that should be integrated into healthcare systems [20, 21]. A number of authoritative reviews and guidelines recommendations have been used on the basis of these [22–31].

Among the more recently published guidelines [30–35] are those of the European Respiratory Society (ERS) Task Force on guidelines for smoking cessation in patients with respiratory diseases [32]. According to these guidelines, patients with respiratory disease have a greater and more urgent need to stop smoking than the average smoker; thus respiratory physicians must take a proactive and continuing role with all smokers in motivating them to stop and in providing treatment to aid smoking cessation. Although the cost of implementing these recommendations will partly be offset by a reduction in attendance for exacerbations, *etc.*, a budget should be established in order to enable implementation

Recommendations and strategies for smoking cessation

In all of these guidelines, there is general agreement about what constitutes effective treatment. The various guidelines consistently recommend that physicians first identify smokers and then motivate them to make an attempt at stopping smoking and support them in quitting successfully through counselling, pharmacotherapy and follow-up.

According to these guidelines, physicians should routinely: assess and record patients' smoking status; advise smokers to quit; assess their readiness to do so; and assist them by offering support themselves or referring them to more intensive specialist support. Figure 1 illustrates effective implementation of smoking cessation strategies using the steps recommended in the current guidelines, based on the five As strategy: ask, advise, assess, assist, and arrange a follow-up.

Two approaches show strong evidence of efficacy for smoking cessation: pharmacotherapy, and counselling. Each is effective by itself, but the two in combination achieve the highest rates of smoking cessation. The efficacy of a treatment correlates with its intensity, but even brief interventions by physicians during an office visit promote smoking cessation. Providing a brief period of counselling (≤ 3 min) is more effective than simply advising the patient to quit and doubles the cessation rate, as compared with no intervention [10, 32, 36].

Numerous effective pharmacotherapies for smoking cessation now exist. Except in the presence of contraindications, these should be used for all patients attempting to quit smoking. First-line pharmacotherapies were identified that reliably increase long-term smoking abstinence rates.

NRT or bupropion SR in conjunction with behavioural intervention for the management of smoking cessation are recommended as the first-line smoking cessation interventions. Two second-line pharmacotherapies have been identified as efficacious, and may be considered by clinicians if first-line pharmacotherapies are ineffective: 1) clonidine, and 2) nortriptyline [10–29].

More recently, a new compound, varenicline, a partial agonist of nicotinic receptors, has shown high effectiveness compared with placebo and bupropion [37–39] regarding smoking abstinence, and is another recommended pharmaceutical option that might be effective as a first-line treatment according to the updated guidelines [33–35].

Except in the presence of contraindications, these drugs should be used in almost all patients attempting to quit smoking. Smokers who smoke >10 cigarettes·day^{-1} and who are ready to stop should be encouraged to use NRT, bupropion or varenicline to aid cessation. Health professionals who deliver smoking cessation interventions should give smokers accurate information and advice regarding these products.

Healthcare delivery systems (including hospitals) are directed to identify patients' smoking status, offer smoking cessation services, and document these actions. The Public Health Service guidelines urge health insurers to cover all recommended treatments, including counselling and pharmacotherapy [10, 12].

The healthcare system should offer treatment as back up to brief opportunistic interventions for those smokers who require more intensive support from smoking cessation clinics. This support can be offered individually or in groups, and should include coping skills training and social support. A well-tested group format includes approximately five sessions of ~1 h over ~1 month with follow-up. Intensive support should include the offer of or encouragement to use pharmacotherapy (as appropriate) and clear advice and instruction regarding how to use it [32–35].

Hospital staff should ask about patients' smoking status prior to or on admission, and offer brief advice and assistance to those interested in stopping. Patients should be advised of the hospital's smoke-free status before admission. Hospital patients who require it should also be offered medication treatment. An intensive programme with weekly visits, personal consultation with the respiratory physician and use of pharmacotherapy can increase the cessation rate of motivated smokers who attempt to quit [40].

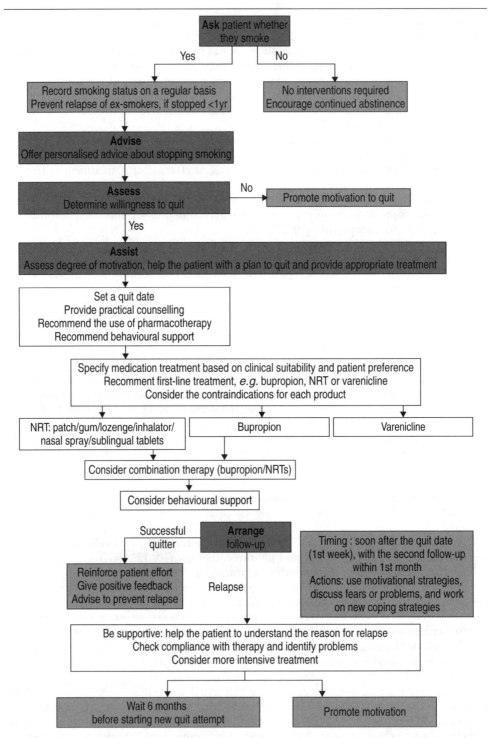

Fig. 1. – Recommended smoking cessation steps and approved first-line interventions. NRT: nicotine replacement therapy.

Telephone helplines can be effective and are very popular with smokers [33, 35]. Although more research is required regarding their effectiveness, they seem likely to provide a valuable service to smokers and should be made available where possible.

Recommendations regarding special populations

Smoking is a complex multifactorial addiction, and the presence of various social and clinical factors can make it harder for some smokers to quit than others. The updated US guidelines [34, 35] address the treatment of tobacco dependence in special populations, such as females, pregnant smokers, racial and ethnic minorities, hospitalised smokers, smokers with comorbid conditions or chemical dependency, children and adolescents, and older smokers.

Special considerations are required for patients who have developed smoking-related cardiovascular disease or COPD [10–12]. These smokers are generally older individuals compared with general populations, have a higher cumulative cigarette consumption and higher nicotine addiction score, and may have a history of depression, all of which reduce the probability of successfully quitting. Smoking cessation is considered the most important therapeutic intervention for COPD and cardiovascular diseases [2, 7, 8]. Pharmacological treatment has been shown to be well tolerated and effective as an aid in smoking cessation in these patients [41–43]. However, a special approach to these patients, with more intensive interventions, may increase more the success rate of smoking cessation. The American Heart Association/American College of Cardiology guidelines for preventing heart attack and death in patients with atherosclerotic cardiovascular disease published in 2001 [29], and more recently specifically for females [44] ERS guidelines for respiratory patients published in 2006 [32] and some other recently published recommendations address strategies for the special smokers population such as those with lung cancer [36, 45] and pregnancy [46].

Conclusions

Since nearly 4 million people globally are estimated to die annually as a result of smoking, reducing the number of current smokers should substantially lower future smoking-related morbidity and mortality. Tobacco users must not be left to stop smoking on their own, and most healthcare professionals should help people who are willing to stop smoking. Additional urgency is required in promoting smoking cessation worldwide. Physicians must realise that nicotine addiction is a chronic condition that requires long-term management with interventions that are extremely cost-effective but underused. Brief counselling advice and specific pharmacological treatment may be implemented effectively in routine medical care. Special care and more intensive interventions may increase the success rate of smoking cessation among smoking patients with chronic diseases.

Summary

Healthcare providers should deliver state-of-the-art assistance to their smoking patients in order to help them to quit.

Given that the health benefits of stopping smoking are enormous, and that significant morbidity, mortality and economic effects are attributed to smoking, a number of smoking cessation guidelines have been published, in recent years, that provide recommendations for interventions and strategies for promoting the treatment of tobacco dependence.

These reviews and guidelines draw on hundreds of well-controlled trials, and emphasise not only that treatment for tobacco dependence is effective but also that it is extremely cost-effective.

The various guidelines consistently recommend that physicians first identify smokers, then motivate them to make an attempt at stopping smoking and support them in quitting successfully through counselling, pharmacotherapy and follow-up.

The following key points can be made regarding medication treatment in smoking cessation.

1) Smokers attempting to quit should be encouraged to use medication to aid cessation, except in the presence of contraindications (evidence level A).

2) NRT, bupropion SR and varenicline are first-line treatments for smoking cessation (evidence level A).

3) Various NRTs (gum, patch, inhaler, nasal spray, lozenge and sublingual tablets) are equally effective as smoking cessation treatments (evidence level A).

4) Combining the nicotine patch with a self-administered form of NRT can be more effective than a single form of NRT (evidence level B).

5) Combined treatment with bupropion SR and NRT might be more effective in heavy smokers (evidence level C), combined treatment with varenicline (no evidence).

6) Both NRT and bupropion SR are effective and well tolerated in smokers with stable cardiovascular disease and in COPD patients (evidence level A). Varenicline might have an additional therapeutic effect as a smoking cessation treatment in these groups (evidence level B).

7) Nortriptyline may be used as a second-line medication to treat tobacco dependence (evidence level B).

8) Regular follow-up visits are important and are linked with a longer-term successful outcome (evidence level B).

Keywords: Guidelines, medications, smoking cessation, tobacco addiction, treatment.

References

1. World Health Organization. Tobacco or Health: a Global Status Report. Geneva, World Health Organization, 1997

2. US Department of Health and Human Services. The Health Benefits of Smoking Cessation: a Report of the Surgeon General. DHHS publication No. (CDC) 90–8416. Washington, DC, US Department of Health and Human Services, Public Health Service, Centers for Disease Control, Center for Chronic Disease Prevention and Health Promotion, Office on Smoking and Health, 1990.

3.   Zhu SH, Melcer T, Sun J, Rosbrook B, Pierce JP. Smoking cessation with and without assistance: a population-based analysis. *Am J Prev Med* 2000; 18: 305–311.

4.   Royal College of Physicians. Nicotine Addiction in Britain. London, Royal College of Physicians, 2000.

5.   Hughes JR, Gulliver SB, Fenwick JW, *et al.* Smoking cessation among self-quitters. *Health Psychol* 1992; 11: 331–335.

6.   Lawrence WF, Smith SS, Baker TB, Fiore MC. Does over-the-counter nicotine replacement therapy improve smokers' life expectancy? *Tob Control* 1998; 7: 364–368.

7.   Scanlon PD, Connett JE, Waller LA, Altose MD, Bailey WC, Buist AS. Smoking cessation and lung function in mild-to-moderate chronic obstructive pulmonary disease. The Lung Health Study. *Am J Respir Crit Care Med* 2000; 161: 381–390.

8.   Global Strategy for the Diagnosis, Management, and Prevention of Chronic Obstructive Pulmonary Disease. NIILBI/WIIO Workshop Report. Bethesda, MD, National Institutes of Health. National Heart, Lung, and Blood Institute, 2000.

9.   Fiore MC, Bailey WC, Cohen SJ, *et al.*, Smoking Cessation. Clinical Practice Guideline No. 18. AHCPR publication No.: 96–0692. Rockville, MD, US Department of Health and Human Services. Public Health Service, Agency for Health Care Policy and Research, 1996.

10.   Fiore MC, Bailey WC, Cohen SJ, *et al.*, Clinical Practice Guideline. Treating Tobacco Use and Dependence. Rockville, US Department of Health and Human Services, Public Health Service, 2000.

11.   The Tobacco Use and Dependence Clinical Practice Guideline Panel, Staff and Consortium Representatives. A clinical practice guideline for treating tobacco use and dependence: A US Public Health Service report. *JAMA* 2000; 283: 3244–3254.

12.   Anderson JE, Jorenby DE, Scott WJ, Fiore MC. Treating tobacco use and dependence: an evidence-based clinical practice guideline for tobacco cessation. *Chest* 2002; 121: 932–941.

13.   Hughes JR, Fiester S, Goldstein MG, Resnick MP, Rock N, Ziedonis D. The American Psychiatric Association practice guidelines for the treatment of patients with nicotine dependence. *Am J Psychiatry* 1996; 153: Suppl., S1–S31.

14.   Raw M, McNeill A, West R. Smoking cessation guidelines for health professionals: a guide to effective smoking cessation interventions for the healthcare system. *Thorax* 1998; 53: Suppl. 5, S1–S19.

15.   West R, McNeill A, Raw M. Smoking cessation guidelines for health professionals: an update. *Thorax* 2000; 55: 987–999.

16.   Department of Health. Smoking Kills. A White Paper on Tobacco. London, The Stationery Office, 1998.

17.   National Institute for Clinical Excellence. Guidance on the Use of Nicotine Replacement Therapy (NRT) and Bupropion for Smoking Cessation. Technology Appraisal Guidance No. 39. London, National Institute for Clinical Excellence, 2002.

18.   National Health Committee. Guidelines for Smoking Cessation. Wellington, Ministry of Health, 1999.

19.   Taylor MC, Dingle JL. Prevention of tobacco-caused disease. *In*: Canadian Task Force on the Periodic Health Examination. Ottawa, Health Canada, 1994; pp. 500–511.

20.   World Health Organization, European partnership to reduce tobacco dependence. WHO Evidence Based Recommendations on the Treatment of Tobacco Dependence. Geneva, World Health Organization, 2001.

21.   Task Force on Community Preventive Services. Recommendations regarding interventions to reduce tobacco use and exposure to environmental tobacco smoke. *Am J Prev Med* 2001; 20: Suppl., 10–15

22.   Hughes JR, Goldstein MG, Hurt RD, Shiffman S. Recent advances in the pharmacotherapy of smoking. *JAMA* 1999; 281: 72–76.

23.   Henningfield JE, Fant RV, Gitchell J, Shiffman S. Tobacco dependence: global public health potential for new medications development and indications. *Ann N Y Acad Sci* 2000; 909: 247–256.

24.   Ragout NAS. Treatment of tobacco use and dependence. *N Engl J Med* 2000; 346: 506–512.

25. Lancaster T, Stead L, Silagy C, Sowden A. Effectiveness of interventions to help people stop smoking: findings from the Cochrane Library. *BMJ* 2000; 321: 355–358.

26. Silagy CA, Stead LF, Lancaster T. Use of systematic reviews in clinical practice guidelines: case study of smoking cessation. *BMJ* 2001; 323: 833–836.

27. Eckert T, Junker C. Motivation for smoking cessation: what role do doctors play? *Swiss Med Wkly* 2001; 131: 521–526.

28. Foulds J. Effectiveness of smoking cessation initiatives. *BMJ* 2002; 324: 608–609.

29. Smith SC Jr, Blair SN, Bonow RO, *et al.* AHA/ACC Guidelines for preventing heart attack and death in patients with atherosclerotic cardiovascular disease: 2001 update. A statement for health professionals from the American Heart Association and the American College of Cardiology. *Circulation* 2001; 104: 1577–1579.

30. Le Foll B, Melihan-Cheinin P, Rostoker G, Lagrue G, Working Group of AFSSAPS. Smoking cessation guidelines: evidence-based recommendations of the French Health Products Safety Agency. *Eur Psychiatry* 2005; 20: 431–441.

31. Bernstein SL, Boudreaux ED, Cydulka RK, *et al.* Tobacco control interventions in the emergency department: a joint statement of emergency medicine organizations. *Ann Emerg Med* 2006; 48: e417–e426.

32. Tønnesen P, Carrozzi L, Fagerström KO, *et al.* Smoking cessation in patients with respiratory diseases: a high priority, integral component of therapy. *Eur Respir J* 2007; 29: 390–417.

33. Bader P, McDonald PW, Selby P. An algorithm for tailoring pharmacotherapy for smoking cessation: results from a Delphi panel of international experts. *Tob Control* 2008; Epub ahead of print.

34. Clinical Practice Guideline Treating Tobacco Use and Dependence 2008 Update Panel, Liaisons, and Staff. A clinical practice guideline for treating tobacco use and dependence: 2008 update. A U.S. Public Health Service report. *Am J Prev Med* 2008; 35: 158–176.

35. Kuehn BM. Updated US smoking cessation guideline advises counseling, combining therapies. *JAMA* 2008; 299: 2736.

36. Dragnev KH, Stover D, Dmitrovsky E. Lung Cancer prevention. The guidelines. *Chest* 2003; 123: Suppl., 60S–71S.

37. Gonzales D, Rennard SI, Nides M, *et al.* Varenicline, an α4β2 nicotinic acetylcholine receptor partial agonist, *vs* sustained-release bupropion and placebo for smoking cessation. A randomized controlled trial. *JAMA* 2006; 296: 47–55.

38. Jorenby DE, Hays JT, Rigotti NA, *et al.* Efficacy of varenicline, an α4β2 nicotinic acetylcholine receptor partial agonist, *vs* placebo or sustained-release bupropion for smoking cessation. A randomized controlled trial. *JAMA* 2006; 296: 56–63.

39. Tonstad S, Tønnesen P, Hajek P, *et al.* Effect of maintenance therapy with varenicline on smoking cessation. A randomized controlled trial. *JAMA* 2006; 296: 64–71.

40. Wolfenden L, Campbell E, Wiggers J, Walsh RA, Bailey L. Helping hospital patients quit: what the evidence supports and what guidelines recommend. *J Prev Med* 2008; 46: 346–357.

41. Tonstad S, Farsang C, Klaene G, *et al.* Bupropion SR for smoking cessation in cardiovascular disease: a multicenter randomised study. *Eur Heart J* 2003; 24: 946–955.

42. Tashkin DP, Kanner R, Bailey W, *et al.* Smoking cessation in patients with chronic obstructive pulmonary disease: a double-blind, placebo-controlled, randomised trial. *Lancet* 2001; 357: 1571–1575.

43. Kanner RE, Connett JE, Williams DE, Buist AS. Effects of randomized assignment to a smoking cessation intervention and changes in smoking habits on respiratory symptoms in smokers with early chronic obstructive pulmonary disease: the Lung Health Study. *Am J Med* 1999; 106: 410–416.

44. Mosca L, Appel LJ, Benjamin EJ, *et al.* Evidence-based guidelines for cardiovascular disease prevention in women. American Heart Association scientific statement. *Arterioscler Thromb Vasc Biol* 2004; 24: e29–e50.

45. Cassileth BR, Deng GE, Gomez JE, Johnstone PA, Kumar N, Vickers AJ. Complementary therapies and integrative oncology in lung cancer. ACCP evidence-based clinical practice guidelines (2nd edition). *Chest* 2007; 132: Suppl., 340S–354S.

46. Coleman T. Recommendations for the use of pharmacological smoking cessation strategies in pregnant women. *CNS Drugs* 2007; 21: 983–993.

CHAPTER 6

Assessment of the patient

K.O. Fagerström

Correspondence: K.O. Fagerström, Smoker's Information Centre, Berga Alle 1, 25452 Helsingborg, Sweden. Fax: 46 42165760; E-mail: karl.fagerstrom@swipnet.se

Smoking status

Usually a direct question is enough. If the patient claims to be a nonsmoker but the therapist is uncertain, CO in exhaled air, cotinine from saliva, urine or blood, and inspection of the patient's fingers and breath can yield valuable information. Smoking status should be noted prominently in the patient's record, including the type of tobacco use (cigarettes, cheroots, cigars or pipe) and the quantity-inclusive cumulative cigarette consumption in pack-years.

Motivation to give up

A willingness or strong motivation to give up seems to be a *sine qua non* for successful cessation of tobacco consumption. No good and validated measure for assessing degree of motivation exists. However, a straightforward means of assessing the patient's willingness to give up smoking can be simply to ask the patient to rate the following on a 10-point scale: "how important is it for you to give up smoking?" The patient can be helped by anchoring the scale with 10 representing extremely important and 0 being of no importance.

In the clinical situation, an idea of the perceived self-efficacy might also be desirable. It may, therefore, be informative to ask the following question. "If you were to decide to stop smoking, how confident are you that you would succeed?" On the 10-point scale, 10 points represents being "entirely certain that I would succeed" and 0 "entirely certain I would fail" [1].

In order to obtain further information on the lack of self-confidence and how it can be strengthened, the physician could ask "you gave me a low 3 for self-confidence, what would need to happen for you to get from your current 3 to a 7". The same sort of question can, of course, be asked about motivation. If the readiness to give up is good, the patient should rate themself highly on both variables. If motivation is high but self-efficacy is low, treatment and support are critical to success. If self-efficacy is high but willingness to try is low, effective health education is critical. If both are low, both motivation and self-efficacy need to be built up, but, if a patient scores highly on both questions, a quit date could be set immediately. It should be understood that motivation to give up is not a slowly changing state but something that can change very fast. A patient who was not motivated at the previous visit could well be willing to try on the current occasion. In addition, many patients have a desire to give up sometime. However, this may be more of a hope than anything else, and such patients may not be ready to give up at a certain visit, but just knowing about a new treatment that sounds appropriate might turn a patient to be ready to quit immediately. Furthermore, some

Eur Respir Mon, 2008, 42, 44–50. Printed in UK - all rights reserved. Copyright ERS Journals Ltd 2008; European Respiratory Monograph; ISSN 1025-448x.

patients who are not willing to try to quit abruptly may be willing to reduce their smoking. Successful reduction can also lead to complete cessation [2].

Dependence

The vast majority of all smokers smoke to a large degree for the effects of nicotine, and many are even dependent upon nicotine. The strength of the dependency varies considerably. In the World Health Organization's international classification of diseases and injuries [3], seven criteria (strong desire to smoke, difficulties in controlling the amount, continued use despite harmful consequences, influencing priorities of other activities, increased tolerance and physical withdrawal) are used to diagnose tobacco dependence. Three of the seven criteria need to be fulfilled for the diagnosis. Using this system, tobacco dependence can only be determined qualitatively. Some work has been carried out so that it can be used as a qualitative scale [4]. However, no standardised data for such use exists.

Historically, number of cigarettes has served as the only measure of dependence. Today, research has shown that simply the number of cigarettes by itself is not an optimal measure of nicotine dependence [5].

Biochemical measures, such as nicotine and its major metabolite cotinine, have more recently been used as indicators of dependence. However, nicotine has a short half-life of ~2 h and its concentrations are, therefore, very dependent upon time of day and when the last cigarette was smoked. Cotinine, a metabolite of nicotine with a half-life of 15–20 h is, therefore, often recommended. Both can be analysed in blood plasma, saliva and urine. For cotinine, concentrations in plasma of <40 $ng \cdot mL^{-1}$ are considered nonsmoking levels, but the majority of nonsmokers not exposed to second-hand smoke have concentrations ranging from unmeasurable up to 10 $ng \cdot mL^{-1}$. The smoker's mean concentration is ~200 $ng \cdot mL^{-1}$ but can be as high as 1,000 $ng \cdot mL^{-1}$ [6].

An indication of degree of dependence can also be obtained using questionnaires. The Fagerström Test for Nicotine Dependence (FTND) is a widely used and researched short (six items) questionnaire [7]. The relevant information can be obtained in an interview or the smokers can fill in the questionnaire (Appendix 1) themselves. The score ranges 0–10, and the mean in representative samples of smokers is usually in the range 3–4 points. The two most important questions concern time to first cigarette in the morning and number of cigarettes. Just these two questions give almost as much information as the whole questionnaire. In conditions of extreme time and space urgency, time to first cigarette alone can be used as a proxy [5]. Another strong but more infrequent indicator of dependence is nocturnal smoking [8]. Such smokers usually score very high on the FTND. The higher the score the stronger the dependence and the more difficult it is to give up. The score also predicts severity of withdrawal and need for pharmacological treatment [9], and is related to genetic determination of certain nicotinic receptors [10]. In Appendix 2, smokers are roughly characterised according to the severity of their dependence.

Another recently published but not yet well-validated scale is the Cigarette Dependence Scale [11].

Earlier smoking cessation experience

It can be valuable to ask about experiences from earlier quit attempts, *e.g.* the duration of the longest period without smoking, the difficulties and withdrawal symptoms, whether any methods were used that helped, what triggered relapse and whether anything positive was experienced during the abstinence. This can give some idea as to potential difficulties and thereby an opportunity to better address them.

Carbon monoxide

Cigarette smoking leads to absorption of many toxins. CO is one of very few that can easily be monitored. The assessment of CO concentration can be seen as an indicator of total smoke intake. The CO concentration in the body can easily be obtained by getting the smoker to exhale into a CO analyser (fig. 1). The CO is measured in parts per million and this can easily be converted into carboxyhaemoglobin (COHb) concentration. In the absence of a CO analyser, COHb can, of course, be obtained from analysis of a blood sample. Demonstration of the CO effect in smokers is of great motivational value. The recommended procedure is for the therapist to first exhale into the device, producing the normal CO concentration of 1–3 ppm. Then the smoker blows into the machine, where they immediately and invariably obtain a much higher reading, usually in the range 10–20 ppm (2–5% COHb). Under normal environmental conditions, a nonsmoker value should not exceed 4 ppm [12].

CO has a half-life of ~4 h and is somewhat exercise-dependent. Readings in the morning are, therefore, much lower than those in the afternoon [10]. CO levels are normal 1 day, or certainly 2 days, after the last cigarette. This rapid normalisation is very rewarding for the subject to observe. After normalisation, CO assessment can be used for monitoring the nonsmoking status, which is usually a good support during follow-up. The abnormal smoking CO level can be used to inform the smoker of the

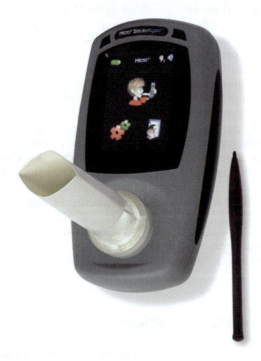

Fig. 1. – Carbon monoxide analyser.

mechanisms by which smoking, and particularly CO itself, contributes to cardiovascular disease.

If the target is reduced smoking rather than cessation, CO monitoring is essential. The number of cigarettes smoked can be reduced but the smoker often compensates for the potential reduction in, for example, nicotine intake by inhaling more effectively from the remaining cigarettes, resulting in little impact upon reduction of health hazards and dependence. Furthermore CO, preferably measured in the afternoon, is also an indicator of dependence. Since there is relatively little variation in the emission of CO from different cigarette brands (contrary to what might be printed on the packs), the differences obtained can largely be ascribed to nicotine-seeking and dependence. Chronic obstructive pulmonary disease (COPD) patients have been found to produce higher CO readings in expired air. Whether this is due to differences in CO half-life, inflammatory production of CO or other intrinsic factors, or simply due to more smoking, is not clear, but it seems likely that more smoking and different inhalation patterns are the most likely explanations for the higher CO levels in COPD patients [13].

Comorbidity

Smoking can be seen as a means of coping with daily life's stress and hassles. It has been observed that, in heavy smokers, there is an aggregation of clinical and subclinical problems, such as schizophrenia, attention deficit–hyperactivity disorder, and other drug dependence and abuse. However, the most researched and relevant psychiatric disorder found in association with smoking is depression [14]. A history of depression and smoking often go together and may share genetic mechanisms [15]. If a smoker presents with a history of depression, it is more difficult for them to give up smoking [16], and their treatment needs to be adjusted accordingly. Depression and anxiety have been found to be very common among respiratory, and particularly COPD, patients [17–19]. In order to better understand and be able to treat the depressed patient, it is recommended that the physician measures depression and low mood. There are some very brief scales, such as the two following questions. 1) During the past month, have you been bothered by feeling down, depressed or hopeless? 2) During the past month, have you often been bothered by having little interest or pleasure in doing things? A yes response to either of these two questions is a strong sign of depression [20].

A single question for assessment of depression (Did you feel down during most days of the last two weeks?) has also been used and been found to have reasonable validity among stroke patients [21]. Other more elaborate tests for depression have also been used, the Anxiety and Depression Scale [22], Hamilton Depression Subscale [23], Primary Care Evaluation of Mental Disorders and Beck Depression Inventory [24].

Concluding remarks

The assessments suggested here are not all equally important. The basic requirements are to determine whether or not the patient is a smoker, what the motivation is for giving up, and the results and experience from possible earlier quit attempts. Dependence should be assessed by taking a CO sample; review of important comorbid conditions is highly recommended but not absolutely necessary.

Spirometry and other measurments relating to the patient's condition might also be used in an opportunistic way but are not covered here.

Summary

Certain assessments of the smoker can be important to make in order to better diagnose and understand the smoker's dependence and what sort of help might best fit the smoking patient. For that purpose, it is important to understand what motivation the patient has for changing the smoking behaviour, their degree of dependence upon tobacco and any possible comorbid condition that interacts with smoking cessation. The instantaneous measurement of carbon monoxide in exhaled air is another assessment that can be very helpful for increasing motivation and checking progress.

Keywords: Carbon monoxide, comorbidity, dependence, motivation, smoking status.

Appendix 1: Assessment questionnaire

How many cigarettes per day have you on average smoked during the last month?
For how many years have you smoked this amount?
How important is it for you to give up smoking? Give a number.
10 is extremely important and 0 of no importance.
If you want to stop, how confident are you that you would succeed?
10 is entirely certain to succeed and 0 is entirely certain to fail.
How many serious attempts to quit smoking have you made?

Fagerström Test for Nicotine Dependence

The details of the Fagerström Test for Nicotine Dependence are shown in table 1.

Table 1. – Fagerström Test for Nicotine Dependence

Question	Response	Points
1) How soon after you wake up do you smoke your first cigarette?	Within 5 min	3
	6–30 min	2
	31–60 min	1
	After 60 min	0
2) Do you find it difficult to refrain from smoking in places where it is forbidden?	Yes	1
	No	0
3) Which cigarette would you hate most to give up?	The first one in the morning	1
	Any other	0
4) How many cigarettes per day do you smoke?	≤10	0
	11–20	1
	21–30	2
	≥31	3
5) Do you smoke more frequently during the first hours after waking than during the rest of the day?	Yes	1
	No	0
6) Do you smoke if you are so ill that you are in bed most of the day?	Yes	1
	No	0
Total score		

Appendix 2: Characteristics of smokers according to score

The characterisation of smokers according to severity of dependence based on FTND score is shown in table 2.

Table 2. – Characterisation of smokers according to severity of dependence

Points	Smokers %	Comments
0–1	20	Very low dependence Few and light withdrawal symptoms Seldom need help to give up
2–3	30	Large group of smokers Certain degree of dependence Difficult withdrawal symptoms can occur Often manage to give up by themselves Medicines can be of help
4–5	30	Large group of smokers Above average dependence Withdrawal symptoms common Medicines often very helpful Risk of smoking-related disorders is real
6–7	15	Strong dependence and withdrawal Likelihood of giving up smoking poor High risk of smoking-related disorders Medicines important, possibly combinations Higher dose and longer duration may be needed Support treatment important Depression and high alcohol intake common
8–10	5	Small group with extreme dependence Chances of giving up are very small Handicapping withdrawal symptoms Support therapy and medicines essential, preferably over long time and in high dose Most have smoking-related disorders Anxiety, depression, pain and alcohol dependence common

References

1. Rollnick S, Mason P, Butler C. Health Behavior Change. A Guide for Practitioners. London, Churchill Livingstone, 1999.
2. Fagerström KO. Can smoking reduction be a way for smokers not interested in quitting to actually quit? *Respiration* 2005; 72: 216–220.
3. World Health Organization. The ICD-10 Classification of Mental and Behavioural Disorders. Geneva, World Health Organization, 1992.
4. Breslau N, Johnson EO. Predicting smoking cessation and major depression in nicotine dependent smokers. *Am J Pub Health* 1999; 90: 1122–1127.
5. Fagerström KO. Time to first cigarette; the best single indicator of tobacco dependence. *Monaldi Arch Chest Dis* 2003; 59: 95–98.
6. Etter JF, Duc TV, Perneger TV. Saliva cotinine levels in smokers and non-smokers. *Am J Epidemiol* 2000; 151: 251–258.
7. Heatherton TF, Kozlowski LT, Frecker RC, Fagerström KO. The Fagerström Test for Nicotine Dependence: a revision of the Fagerström Tolerance Questionnaire. *Br J Addict* 1991; 86: 1119–1127.
8. Rieder A, Kunze U, Groman E, Kiefer I, Schoberberger R. Nocturnal sleep-disturbing nicotine craving: a newly described symptom of extreme nicotine dependence. *Acta Med Austriaca* 2001; 28: 21–22.

9. Fagerström KO, Schneider N. Measuring nicotine dependence: a review of the Fagerström Tolerance Questionnaire. *J Behav Med* 1989; 12: 159–182.

10. Batra A, Gelfort G, Bartels M. The dopamine D2 receptor (*DRD2*) gene – a genetic risk factor in heavy smoking? *Addict Biol* 2000; 5: 431–438.

11. Etter J-F, Le Houezec J, Perneger TV. A self-administered questionnaire to measure addiction to cigarettes: the Cigarette Dependence Scale. *Neuropsychopharmacology* 2003; 28: 359–370.

12. Javors MA, Hatch JP, Lamb R. Cut-off levels for breath carbon monoxide as a marker for cigarette smoking. *Addiction* 2005; 100: 159–167.

13. Jimenez-Ruiz CA. Smoking characteristics: differences in attitudes and dependence between healthy smokers and smokers with COPD. *Chest* 2001; 119: 1365–1370.

14. Hughes JR. Comorbidity and smoking. *Nicotine Tob Res* 1999; 1: S149–S152.

15. Dierker LC, Avenevoli S, Stolar M, Merikangas KR. Smoking and depression: an examination of mechanisms of comorbidity. *Am J Psychiatry* 2002; 159: 947–953.

16. Glassman AH, Covey LS, Stetner F, Rivelli S. Smoking cessation and the course of major depression: a follow up study. *Lancet* 2001; 357: 1929–1932.

17. Wagena E, Kant I, Huibersd MJ, *et al.* Psychological distress and depressed mood in employees with asthma, chronic bronchitis or emphysema: a population-based observational study on prevalence and the relationship with smoking cigarettes. *Eur J Epidemiol* 2004; 19: 147–153.

18. Borson S, Calypoole K, McDonald GJ. Depression and chronic obstructive pulmonary disease: treatment trials. *Semin Clin Neuropsychiatry* 1998; 3: 115–130.

19. Jordan N, Lee TA, Valenstein M, Weiss KB. Effect of care setting on evidence-based depression treatment for veterans with COPD and comorbid depression. *J Gen Intern Med* 2007; 10: 1447–1452.

20. Arroll B, Khin N, Kerse N. Screening for depression in primary care with two verbally asked questions: cross sectional study. *BMJ* 2003; 327: 1144–1146.

21. Watkins C, Daniels L, Jack C, Dickinson H, van der Broek M. Accuracy of a single question in screening for depression in a cohort of patients after stroke: comparative study. *BMJ* 2001; 323: 1159.

22. Moroni L, Bettinardi O, Vidotto G, *et al.* Scheda ansia e depressione forma ridotta: norme per l'utilizzo in ambito riabilitativo. [Anxiety and Depression Short Scale: norms for its use in rehabilitation.]. *Monaldi Arch Chest Dis* 2006; 66: 255–263.

23. Stage KB, Middelboe T, Pisinger C. Measurment of depression in patients with chronic obstructive disease. *Nord J Psychiatry* 203, 57: 297–301.

24. Kunik ME, Azzam PN, Ouchek J, *et al.* A practical screening tool for anxiety and depression in patients with chronic breathing disorders. *Psychosomatics* 2007; 48: 16–21.

CHAPTER 7

The stage-of-change model in smoking cessation in respiratory patients: does it need to be revisited?

G. Barbano, M.C. Bressan, S. Nardini

Pulmonary and TB Unit, General Hospital, Vittorio Veneto, Italy.

Correspondence: S. Nardini, Pulmonary and TB Unit, General Hospital, ULSS 7, Via Forlanini, 71, 31029 Vittorio Veneto, Treviso, Italy. E-mail: snardini@qubisoft.it

Smoking cessation is the first and most important intervention in the prevention and treatment of respiratory diseases. However, there are many obstacles to reaching this goal that may affect both the diagnosis and treatment of smokers.

Smoking is an addiction [1, 2], although it differs from that to illicit drugs; education and training are necessary to the treatment of smokers, as to that of any other disease. However, current students of medicine rarely find smoking cessation included in their curricula, and past students did not find it at all [3].

For this reason, physicians were not so ready to quiz their patients about their smoking (as it was regarded as a behaviour rather than a disease) in the (recent) past, but, over the last few years, things have changed and the majority of health professionals have now realised the importance of their intervention in their patients' smoking.

The current guidelines (*e.g.* [4]) state that the motivation to quit is the prerequisite for starting a smoking cessation attempt. Indeed, smoking cessation starts with identification of smokers among patients, continues with the analysis of the smoker's character and the prescription of adequate treatment, and finally ends (or continues the cycle) with follow-up. However, after having ascertained the current smoking status of a patient, and having recommended cessation, the very critical point follows, consisting of determination of their willingness to quit; if the patient is not motivated, the intervention should be delayed.

This model has two important implications for physicians. It implies that quitting smoking is a sequential process, and, consequently, the physician's task is to help the patient to move through it without leaps, and must wait to treat the smoker until they are motivated.

The present chapter deals with the issue of motivation and analyses the problems arising from the current suggested approach when coping with a smoker suffering from a respiratory disease.

What is motivation?

Generally speaking, to be motivated means to be activated to take an action. Motivation explains not only what someone decides to do but also the strength of their decision.

Eur Respir Mon, 2008, 42, 51–56. Printed in UK - all rights reserved. Copyright ERS Journals Ltd 2008; European Respiratory Monograph; ISSN 1025-448x.

The motivation to quit is the intention to start a quit attempt not generically in the future but immediately or on a definite, close enough, date. It is defined by a positive answer to the question (asked by the physician) "are you willing to try to quit now?"

If the patient answers "yes" to this question, guidelines suggest that treatment is started immediately (directly, if the physician is fit to the task, or following referral of the patient to a clinic if not).

If the patient answers "no", then an intervention is suggested to increase motivation in the future, in order to maximise the probability that an attempt is started in the future.

These suggestions come from the transtheoretical model of J.O. Prochaska and C.C. DiClemente [5]. According to this model, the process of quitting smoking should be included into a cycle of changes. This cycle comprises four different stages. During the first stage, pre-contemplation, the behaviour is perfectly satisfying to the patient and they feel no need to change. During the second stage, contemplation, the need for a change is sensed, but not so strongly as to promote action and no plan is made for the near future. During the third stage, preparation, the patient has decided to try to change their habit/behaviour and is prepared to start the attempt in the immediate future; in this stage, they can fix a date for the beginning of such an attempt. During the fourth stage, action, the patient starts their attempt.

Even if there is no standard means of measuring motivation, it is suggested that the patient be tested with some questions that can indicate what their feelings are about smoking (for instance, in Italy, the most usual way is to present the patient with a wheel divided into four parts (the four stages) and ask them where they consider themselves to be), and then to set a date for starting quitting and helping the patient with behavioural and pharmacological interventions. Treatment should be refrained from if the patient is in the contemplation or pre-contemplation stage.

For others, a motivational interview is suggested (defined as a "client-centred, directive method for enhancing intrinsic motivation to change by exploring and resolving ambivalence" in [6]), but this is a time-consuming tool, to be used by skilled psychologists.

If a physician thinks that a motivational interview might be of use, then they can address the patient in a formal psychological consultation. However, it is the present authors' opinion that it is more important to give an idea of how to approach a smoker with a respiratory problem to a chest physician than to create amateur psychologists

To this end, for chest physicians the suggestion of treating only motivated people seems not to be the best solution for patients suffering from a respiratory disease, for which smoking is often the underlying cause and always the most important factor in worsening.

In such cases, is there room for other different approaches?

Approaching the smoker

In respiratory medicine, it is rare that a patient who has presented with a respiratory complaint and is a current smoker immediately answers "yes" to the question regarding whether they want to attempt quitting immediately. If patients are evaluated according to the stage-of-change model, most of them are categorised as far from motivated. In a series of chronic obstructive pulmonary disease patients attending the present authors' clinic, only 8.9% of patients were in the preparation stage, whereas 60.7% were in the contemplation stage and 29.4% in the pre-contemplation stage [7].

If guidelines are followed, this means that only one out of ten patients will attempt to quit; the other nine will be treated, at best, with a certain delay. In other words, the physician again risks doing nothing for their smoker patient; some years ago the physician did nothing because they were not educated on the subject, and today because their patient is not motivated.

However, if the prospect of doing nothing is unfavourable, the next step could be to address the following questions. Is the transtheoretical model useful in smoking cessation, at least in a chest clinic? Is it the only guide available for treating smoker patients? How can a chest physician best approach a smoker?

In smoking cessation, the model of J.O. Prochaska and C.C. DiClemente has been much questioned, especially in recent years. The definition of the stages is somehow generic and cannot be measured, meaning that the staging itself can often be viewed as arbitrary [8]. Furthermore, it seems to predict the attempt but not its success (cessation), the latter being better predicted by nicotine dependence and self-efficacy [9].

In two highly intriguing papers, LARABIE [10] and WEST and SOHAL [11] found that, in their sample of smokers, more than a half and slightly less than a half, respectively, of attempts to stop were made without previous planning. Furthermore, in the latter study, the unplanned quit attempts were more successful than the planned ones.

If the transtheoretical model is not a good guide, an alternative model is proposed in the latter paper, based on catastrophe theory. According to this theory, a system can accumulate a certain grade of tension such that an event, although small, can trigger a sudden and large (catastrophic) change. Referring to behaviour, the past history of the patient can be the basis for a sort of motivational tension such that a trigger, even occasional, can lead to change.

This alternative model is much more appealing for chest physicians, not only because it seems to fit better with the observed situations but also because it maximises their role in smoking cessation; if an occasional event can give a patient the decisive boost, then the consultation or hospitalisation might be that event.

Conversely, the decision to start an attempt to quit smoking can be delayed or hindered by fear of failure, which can be crippling if some (or many) unsuccessful attempts have been made in the past. Thus, in discussing how the doctor can push the patient, it is necessary to consider how the patient will use the boost received. For this consideration, the concept of self-efficacy, elaborated by BANDURA [12], can be useful. According to this concept, how people behave can be predicted by the beliefs they hold about their capabilities; self-esteem and, above all, self-efficacy perception can lead the physician to forecast what their patients will do with the knowledge and skills that they have. This kind of approach leads the doctor to bypass simple observation of their patient's motivation to consider the reasons behind it, so creating the conditions for an active intervention rather than passive observation.

Self-efficacy is used widely in medicine in order to understand and modify health behaviour, for instance in considering physical activity in older people [13] or predicting the level of physical activity in youngsters [14]. Self-efficacy can also be increased to change addictive behaviour [15], but, to the chest physician, it is important to learn to recognise this characteristic in their smokers in order to make the best use of the relationship started with the consultation for a chest disease. Indeed, some hints can be obtained from the simple history of the patient as it is routinely collected for clinical purposes.

In practice, the suggestion to the chest physician is to disregard the transtheoretical model of the stages of change and base their own intervention on usual medical practice (every disease is to be treated) and on the two theories, catastrophe theory and self-efficacy theory.

From this perspective, what is the best approach? How far can a physician go in pushing their nonmotivated patient to a quit attempt? First of all, the limits of a physician's intervention should be known. If they decide to wait for a better disposition of the patient, the risk (or effect) is to waste precious time and give the patient the idea that smoking is, after all, not so important to the doctor. If they decide to intervene at all costs, the risk is to elicit a totally negative attitude from the patient.

As pointed out in another chapter of the present Monograph, the problem is that studies are lacking on smoking cessation among respiratory patients, and most of the scientific literature on smoking cessation comes from the preventive experience, in which healthy smokers who want to quit are assisted.

From these studies, it is known that the probabilities that an attempt will be carried out and will be successful are higher the higher the motivation to quit is (but, as seen above, some authors are questioning this). Failure is frustrating for either patients or physicians, and, if an attempt fails, years will pass before another attempt is started. From less-recent studies, it is known that an attempt was made at a mean of every 3.5 yrs in the USA [16]. It is possible that, as time goes by and attitudes towards smoking change, the number of quit attempts each smoker puts into practice will also increase. In 2005, for instance, an attempt was reported at a mean of every year in the UK [17]. Even if, as is probably the case, every country requires its own data, it is possible to have as a working hypothesis that an attempt is made spontaneously once a year.

A healthy smoker loses 3 months of life expectancy for every year that they continue smoking, and so ≥1 yr of delay means much in terms of disease and suffering. However, with every puff of smoking, a respiratory patient loses not only years of life expectancy but also breath and quality of life.

Conversely, there are also risks in forcing a patient into a quit attempt not supported by motivation. The risks are: 1) the direction of the physician is not followed, thus generating senses of guilt and a fall in self-esteem or disruption of the patient–doctor relationship; or 2) the direction is complied with and the quit attempt is started and failed, thus generating further frustration, and a greater fall in self-esteem and self-efficacy. Therefore, an accurate balance is necessary in order to weigh up the pros and cons of a directive approach, and the risks of drop-outs and even distrust towards the physician should always be borne in mind.

That a patient cannot be obliged to undergo a medical treatment is obvious; however, a chest physician never gives up (or does not start) a treatment (i.e. drugs for tuberculosis or surgical intervention for lung cancer) simply because their patient is initially unwilling to comply with medical advice. Instead, further interviews are carried out, to listen to the patient's beliefs and to convince them.

The approach to the smoker respiratory patient has surely been hampered by the fact that smoking is perceived neither by the patient nor by the majority of doctors as representing so great a danger as tuberculosis or cancer. However, it can be facilitated by the fact that an illness, especially if an acute respiratory one (or an acute exacerbation of a chronic respiratory condition), can be the best push to quit, since the patient usually decides to, or is obliged to, stop, or significantly reduce, their smoking due to their respiratory condition.

Therefore, before dropping this therapeutic option, every attempt should be made to discuss with the patient the reasons in favour of the physician's suggestions, the patient's fears and opinions, and the outcomes which can be expected from the intervention, bearing in mind that, difficult as it can be, treating respiratory patients for cessation is not impossible.

In considering the interview with a respiratory patient who is a smoker, the most important point for the physician to remember is that the patient probably feels depressed and guilty for their situation. The patient knows that they ought to stop but their smoking is absolutely necessary to them. They have certainly already been told to quit lots of times, and, since they have not succeeded, are experiencing low self-esteem and very low confidence.

The physician, when facing these feelings, usually reacts by reinforcing their advice to stop, by emphasising the reasons why quitting is advisable; however, in this way, which is just a repetition of a long-lasting story, the patient can react negatively. On the contrary, the physician should understand the feelings of the patient and let them realise that the physician's aim is to help rather than to judge.

At the same time, if the patient has been told to quit, they have surely never been treated for smoking cessation with behavioural and/or pharmacological treatment; they have usually tried on their own. Smoking cessation, however prescribed, is to be delivered as part of the general treatment of the respiratory patient [18]. From this perspective, the best approach, in such cases, seems to be not to use the stage-of-change model to decide whether or not to start therapy, but rather as a prognostic tool, similarly to what can be done in asthma, in which certain types of patient (young and careless, for instance) have a poor prognosis as regards compliance to therapy and completely successful disease control.

The operational suggestion, detailed more in another chapter of the present Monograph, is to treat the patient with harm (or risk) reduction. This means that, if the patient does not want to start an immediate attempt, the doctor can negotiate a reduction in the number of cigarettes smoked per day (usually proposed by the patient themself), with the final goal of cessation, or, if impossible, lifelong sustained reduction.

In summary, the chest physician has to approach the respiratory patient suffering from smoking no differently than a patient with any other disease, *i.e.* obtaining diagnosis and staging, prescribing evidence-based treatments and monitoring the results, doing everything in a sensible way, which takes into account the personality and past history of the patient. The most important message is that smoking should not be considered as different from any other chronic disease that the physician faces in everyday practice.

References

1. World Health Organization. International Statistical Classification of Diseases and Related Health Problems. 10th Revision. Vol. 1. F17. Mental and Behavioural Disorders due to Use of Tobacco. Geneva, World Health Organization, 1992.
2. American Psychiatric Association. Diagnosis and Statistical Manual of Mental Disorders. 4th Edn, revised. Washington, DC, American Psychiatric Association, 1994.
3. Richmond R. Teaching medical students about tobacco. *Thorax* 1999; 54: 70–78.
4. Agency for Health Care Policy and Research. Treating Tobacco Use and Dependence: 2008 Update. Clinical Interventions for Tobacco Use and Dependence. www.ncbi.nlm.nih.gov/books/bv.fcgi?rid=hstat2.section.28251
5. Prochaska JO, Velicer WF. The transtheoretical model of health behaviour change. *Am J Health Promot* 1997; 12: 38–48.
6. Miller WR, Rollnick S. Motivational Interviewing: Preparing People for Change. 2nd Edn. New York, Guilford Press, 2002.
7. Barbano G, Diamandi A, Nardini S. In Respiratory Patients Short Term Complete Abstinence from Smoking does not Depend on the Stage of Change. www.ers-education.org/pages/default.aspx?id=335
8. West R. Time for a change: putting the transtheoretical (stages of change) model to rest. *Addiction* 2005; 100: 1036–1039.

9.   Hyland A, Borland R, Li Q, *et al.* Individual-level predictors of cessation behaviours among participants in the International Tobacco Control (ITC) Four Country Survey. *Tob Control* 2006; 15: Suppl. 3, iii83–iii94.

10. Larabie LC. To what extent do smokers plan quit attempts? *Tob Control* 2005; 14: 425–428.

11. West R, Sohal T. "Catastrophic" pathways to smoking cessation: findings from national survey. *BMJ* 2006; 332: 458–460.

12. Bandura A. Self-efficacy. *In*: Ramachaudran VS, ed. Encyclopedia of Human Behaviour. Vol. 4. New York, Academic Press, 1994; pp. 71–81. (Reprinted *In*: Friedman H, ed. Encyclopedia of Mental Health. San Diego, Academic Press, 1998.)

13. Lee LL, Arthur A, Avis M. Using self-efficacy theory to develop interventions that help older people overcome psychological barriers to physical activity: a discussion paper. *Int J Nurs Stud* 2008; 45: 1690–1699.

14. Valois RF, Umstattd MR, Zullig KJ, Paxton RJ. Physical activity behaviors and emotional self-efficacy: is there a relationship for adolescents? *J Sch Health* 2008; 78: 321–327.

15. Hyde J, Hankins M, Deale A, Marteau TM. Interventions to increase self-efficacy in the context of addiction behaviours: a systematic literature review. *J Health Psychol* 2008; 13: 607–623.

16. Hughes JR. Four beliefs that may impede progress in the treatment of smoking. *Tob Control* 1999; 8: 323–326.

17. Lader D, Goddard E. Smoking Related Attitudes and Behaviour, 2004. London, Office of National Statistics, 2005.

18. Tønnesen P, Carrozzi L, Fagerström KO, *et al.* Smoking cessation in patients with respiratory diseases: a high priority, integral component of therapy. *Eur Respir J* 2007; 29: 390–417.

CHAPTER 8

How to communicate with the smoking patient

K.O. Fagerström

Correspondence: K.O. Fagerström, Smoker's Information Centre, Berga Alle 1, 25452 Helsingborg, Sweden. Fax: 46 42165760; E-mail: karl.fagerstrom@swipnet.se

Most lung physicians simply have too short a time to spend with their patients, often no more than a few minutes per patient. In order to be efficient with the little time available, the doctor feels a need to use that time to convey important information to the patient, often in an authoritative one-way manner. This style is generally the most effective means of transferring information when little time is available. However, if the aim is to change attitudes, in this case to increase willingness and motivation to change smoking habits, it may not be ideal. Attitudes, and in particular to smoking, a drug use that most smokers like and many identify positively with, are more difficult to change than, for example, learning to avoid allergens. Thus a different strategy is required, particularly since lung patients do not usually approach the physician asking for help to stop smoking. Unfortunately, a common background is that the patient has already been advised several times by the physician or other colleagues and has failed repeatedly. These repeated failures may have eaten so badly into the patient's self-esteem and self-confidence that, in order to obtain a better balance between attitude and actual behaviour, they may say that they are no longer willing to stop. This can simply be seen as accommodating reality, with no thought of trying again when they will fail anyway.

In order to best help such smokers, the physician/therapist needs to establish a good rapport with the smoker, for whom smoking is a very important and sensitive topic. Normally, the patient expects the physician to tell the patient to stop smoking in a direct and clear way that makes the patient embarrassed, and sometimes covertly, if not overtly, aggressive and defensive. Therefore, an approach whereby smoking can be discussed in an unthreatening, respectful and empathic way is called for.

One aim of the conversation with the patient is to gather information regarding the current situation. In order for that to occur, listening becomes an important skill for the physician. The physician could begin by giving the patient a chance to talk about something unthreatening, *e.g.* what they like or dislike about smoking. The patient should be encouraged to talk and provide information about their thoughts on smoking by the physician actively listening and maybe rephrasing or reflecting back what has been said if the patient needs a stimulus to continue talking. The physician should attempt to let the patient discover what could be good about stopping or reducing smoking by asking, for example, "would there be any benefits to your health if you did not smoke at all?" Patients are generally better persuaded by reasons which they feel they have discovered themselves than by those put into their minds by others, including their physician. There are also things that should be avoided as much as possible. The doctor should not rush over too many areas nor attempt to get patients to set a quit date when they are not motivated to do so. This can have negative effects and contribute to what, in all likelihood, will be another failure, which can further damage the patient's fragile self-confidence. In addition, the physician should avoid blaming and placing guilt

Eur Respir Mon, 2008, 42, 57–60. Printed in UK - all rights reserved. Copyright ERS Journals Ltd 2008; European Respiratory Monograph; ISSN 1025-448x.

on the patient, even if it seems legitimate. This is rarely productive. Further, it is important not to be too active in transferring information since the patient can become overloaded. Finally, whatever information and advice is given, the patient should not be preached at. The approach to the patient outlined here is sometimes called motivational interviewing and can be used as a means of changing behaviour in general [1], but has often been used for addictive behaviours in general [2], and tobacco dependence in particular [3].

It is important to understand motivation for quitting and self-confidence in quitting, two constructs that can provide important information about the patient's readiness for and the possibility of actually quitting. The degree of motivation to quit can be seen as the strength of the drive which the smoker has to free themself from smoking. It can also be seen as something that buffers the inevitable suffering that occurs when giving up. Self-confidence is also very important since someone hardly approaches something with maximum effort it they think they will fail. In order to rapidly obtain some understanding concerning motivation and self confidence, the physician could ask "how important is it for you to stop smoking?", and "assuming that you made up your mind to give up smoking, how confident are you that you would succeed?" Both questions should be answered on a 10-point scale, with 10 corresponding to extremely important and entirely certain. This would provide a picture of how the smoker views a quit attempt and what needs to be strengthened. Sometimes, the patient is low in both motivation and self-confidence, in which case encouraging the patient to make a quit attempt may not be a good idea. More often with lung patients, their motivation is probably reasonably strong but their self-confidence in their ability to quit is low. In order to obtain further information regarding the lack of self-confidence and how it can be strengthened, the physician could ask "you gave me a low 3 for self-confidence, what would need to happen for you to get from your current 3 to a 7?" The same sort of question can, of course, be asked about motivation. If the readiness to give up is good, the patient should rate themself highly on both variables.

Figure 1 shows an algorithm that can serve as a practical tool for intervention. The first step in this algorithm is to establish whether or not the patient smokes. This can be assessed by simply asking "do you smoke?". "Do you smoke?" is better than "are you a smoker?" since those smoking just a few cigarettes per day may not see themselves as smokers. If the answer is yes, the next question can go something like "have you ever thought about quitting?"

If the patient has not thought about quitting, the physician is most probably talking to a patient that has a positive attitude towards smoking. Soft questions to follow up with can be "what do you like most about smoking?" and "can you imagine any advantage of not smoking?"

If the smoker has thought about quitting, it is possible to go further by asking "why have you thought about quitting?" It can be important that the patient is stimulated to give reasons as to why quitting is desirable rather than the physician putting the arguments into the smoker's mouth. After reinforcing the reasons for quitting, the next question could be "have you ever tried to quit?"

If the smoker has tried, the natural continuation can be "tell me about your attempts". Information may be obtained here that is pertinent to future quit attempts. Another question to ask can be "what did you like about not smoking?" The physician should try to stimulate the smoker to remember, or, if the attempt was too short, imagine what could have been positive.

When the smoker has thought about quitting but not tried to give up, it can be because they think it is too difficult. The doctor should try to discover what could increase their self-confidence.

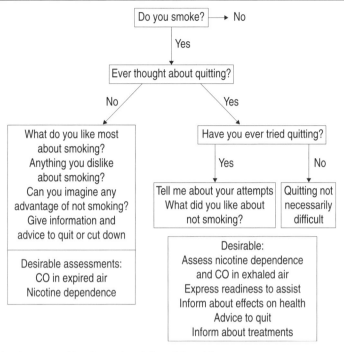

Fig. 1. – Algorithm for approaching the smoker. Adapted from [1].

In summary, the challenge in talking with smokers is to let them, rather than the physician, do most of the talking. They should just be given small prompts to keep them on relevant subjects, and the physician should try to be respectful, understanding and empathic.

Summary

Physicians are normally constrained for time and may need to be very effective in their communication with patients. This often results in directive one-way communication. Such a communication style does not work so well when the objective is behaviour change, especially not with a drug addiction that the patient may like and identify with. One of the goals of motivational communication is to establish a good rapport. This is more likely to occur if the communication does not take the form of direct orders and the use of guilt and blame is avoided. It is important that the physician be understanding and empathic. It is preferable that the patients do most of the talking and that the physicians steer the conversation into relevant areas, with open questions and reinforcing remarks. This style of communication is often referred to as motivational interviewing. An algorithm showing how a smoker can be managed using this style is included.

Keywords: Communication skills, motivational interviewing.

References

1. Rollnick S, Mason P, Butler C. Health Behaviour Change: a Guide for Practitioners. London, Churchill Livingstone, 1999.
2. Miller JH, Moyers T. Motivational interviewing in substance abuse. *Occup Med* 2002; 17: 51–65.
3. Butler CC, Rollnick S, Cohen D, Bachman M, Russell I, Scott N. Motivational consulting *versus* brief advice for smokers in general practice: a randomized trial. *Br J Gen Pract* 1999; 49: 611–616.

CHAPTER 9

Psychological and behavioural interventions for smoking cessation

C.A. Jiménez-Ruiz

Smokers' Clinic, Institute of Public Health, Madrid, Spain.

Correspondence: C.A. Jiménez-Ruiz, C/Santa Cruz del Marcenado, 9 Piso 2, 28015 Madrid, Spain. Fax: 34 912044972; E-mail: carlos.jimenez@salud.madrid.org

Behavioural treatment is a cornerstone of the treatment of tobacco dependence. In the present chapter, the psychological and behavioural interventions for smoking cessation are reviewed. Behavioural interventions can be used singly, in combination or along with drug therapies. There is evidence that combining behavioural interventions with pharmacological treatment significantly increases success rates. Thus smokers who want to make a serious attempt at quitting should be encouraged to use both psychological and pharmacological treatment.

The following interventions can be included as psychological and behavioural strategies to aid smoking cessation: self-help programmes, brief advice, counselling, behavioural advice, biomedicinal risk assessments, and other complementary interventions. During the course of the present chapter, the definitions, procedures and efficacy of these interventions are reviewed.

Self-help programmes

Self-help is defined as structured programming for smokers trying to quit without intensive contact with the therapist. This includes written materials, audio or video tapes, and computer programmes. Self-help programmes can be standard or tailored.

A Cochrane meta-analysis identified 60 trials [1]. In 11 trials in which self-help was compared to no intervention, there was a pooled effect that just reached significance (odds ratio (OR) 1.24; 95% confidence interval (CI) 1.07–1.45). Four further trials in which the control group received alternative written materials did not show evidence of an effect of the smoking self-help materials. The meta-analysis did not find evidence of benefit from adding self-help materials to face-to-face advice, or to nicotine replacement therapy. There were 17 trials using materials tailored for the characteristics of individual smokers, for which meta-analysis supported a small benefit of tailored materials (OR 1.42; 95% CI 1.26–1.61). Taking into account these results, the authors of the meta-analysis concluded as follows [1]. "Standard self-help materials may increase quit rates compared to no intervention, but the effect is likely to be small. Self-help materials do not have an additional benefit when used alongside other interventions such as advice from a healthcare professional or nicotine replacement therapy. There is evidence that materials that are tailored for individual smokers are effective, and are more effective than untailored materials, although the absolute size of effect is still small."

Eur Respir Mon, 2008, 42, 61–73. Printed in UK - all rights reserved. Copyright ERS Journals Ltd 2008; European Respiratory Monograph; ISSN 1025-448x.

Clinicians should consider that self-help materials are an easy intervention and should be readily available in the office and offered to all smokers. Tailored self-help materials can be recommended for smoking cessation.

Brief advice

Brief advice, given by health professionals, can be defined as routinely providing smokers with brief information to help them quit smoking. This information should be delivered opportunistically during routine consultations with smokers whether or no they are seeking help with stopping smoking.

Review of the effectiveness of brief advice given by physicians or nurses suggests the following [2, 3]. 1) Brief physician advice has a significant, albeit small, effect. Studies have shown a small but significant increase in the odds of quitting (OR 1.56; 95% CI 1.32–1.84). This equates to an absolute difference in the cessation rate of ∼2.5% in the group who received medical advice compared with those who did not. It can be calculated that, following brief advice to 50 patients, there will be one extra quitter after 6–12 months. This advice appears to have its effect by triggering a quit attempt rather than by the increasing the chances of success of quit attempts. 2) Increasing the number of advice sessions does not result in a significant increase in efficacy. 3) A very small effect of nursing quit advice of 1% compared to control groups has been found.

Physicians and other health professionals should assess and record the smoking status of their patients at least annually. In patients with smoking-related disorders, more frequent assessment is recommended. After asking about smoking, physicians should give advice to quit.

Health professionals should bear in mind that the way in which smoking should be asked about depends upon who is asking the question and in what situation it is being asked. These professionals should use their clinical skills to carry out this assessment appropriately. When the smoker turns up in the office for the first time, the question could be asked directly and then advice against smoking provided. The way of providing it also differs. In those who have never been advised, short (no more than 2–3 min) and clear advice might be effective. However, those who have been advised several times previously can be fed up with further familiar boring advice and reject it. Thus, with these smokers, the physician's strategy should be different. Trying to establish an open and friendly conversation with the patient should be the best option. In such cases, it is better to try to get the patient to discover the potential benefits of stopping smoking rather than the physician explaining all of the benefits that they can obtain from quitting to them.

In order to increase the efficacy of their brief advice, physicians should take teachable moments into consideration. Teachable moments are defined as events that motivate patients to change and stop risky behaviours [4]. The key role of the clinician in capitalising on any teachable moment lies in personalising the health risk by making the patient aware that a symptom or a disease is directly associated with the patient's smoking and then personalising the benefits of stopping. Clinicians should take advantage of the following teachable moments: when the smoker is suffering from coughing or wheezing, when the smoker comes to a consultation for chest radiography results, and when the physician is making a physical examination of the patient or taking their blood pressure. Pregnancy and hospitalisation are two relevant teachable moments that should be kept in mind. Physicians should not miss the opportunity of giving appropriate advice against smoking to pregnant females, or even to those who want to become pregnant. Hospitalisation, particularly for a heart attack, is one of the best teachable moments. It should be taken into consideration that, for those smokers who have suffered from a myocardial infarction, stopping smoking reduces the risk of having another one to that of a nonsmoker in ~3 yrs [5].

Brief advice from physicians should be more positive than negative. When physicians advise their patients to stop smoking, the positive effects of quitting should be emphasised; nevertheless, the negative effects need also to be explained.

In conclusion, positive brief advice delivered opportunistically by physicians to smokers during routine consultations, taking advantage of teachable moments, is effective in helping smokers to quit and should always be provided to all smokers who are seen in the office.

Counselling

Regarding the manner in which counselling is provided and the time required, there are four types of counselling: individual, group, telephone, and internet interventions.

Individual counselling

This is defined as a face-to-face encounter between a smoking patient and a counsellor trained in assisting smoking cessation. The time spent in contact with the patient is always short.

According to the latest review [6], there is sufficient evidence to support individual counselling for smoking cessation. The abstinence rate is 7% (95% CI 3–10%). It can be calculated that 25 patients require individual counselling in order to gain one extra quitter [6].

Group counselling

When smokers have the opportunity to choose between group and individual therapy, most of them show a preference for one-to-one intervention. Nevertheless, it should be taken into consideration that group therapy offers individuals the opportunity to learn behavioural techniques for smoking cessation and to provide each other with mutual support. Using this kind of support permits more people to be treated by a therapist and could be more cost-effective than individual counselling.

There are some circumstances in which group intervention could be rejected. These include: smokers with behavioural problems, smokers who cannot communicate fully within the group, smokers who cannot attend at the time and date of the scheduled visits, smokers with physical problems that impede them from attending the office, and smokers who are fearful of group treatment.

The latest Cochrane review [7] found a total of 55 trials. Of these, 16 studies compared a group programme with a self-help programme. There was an increase in cessation with the use of a group programme (OR 2.04; 95% CI 1.60–2.60). In an evaluation of seven trials, group programmes were found to be more effective than no intervention controls (OR 2.17; 95% CI 1.37–3.45). There was no evidence that group therapy was more effective than a similar intensity of individual counselling. There was limited evidence that the addition of group therapy to other forms of treatment, such as advice from a health professional or nicotine replacement, produced extra benefit [7].

Running group treatment requires particular experience and skills. It is recommended that two health professionals conduct the group. There are two approaches to conducting a group. One is didactic, with the health professionals acting as teachers and imparting information regarding how to achieve and maintain abstinence from smoking. The other one seeks mutual support among group members in order to achieve abstinence. Table 1 shows a schedule for group treatment and the objectives of each visit. [8]. The inclusion of social support in a group intervention by means of pairing smokers to provide each other with mutual support (buddy condition) has not been proven efficacious. In a recent study, 563 smokers attending groups at a smokers' clinic were randomised to either a buddy condition or receipt of the same treatment without the buddy component. Smokers in the buddy condition were no more likely than smokers in the control condition to remain abstinent at 1, 4 or 26 weeks (OR 1.45; 95% CI 0.92–2.29; p=0.06) [9]. Moreover, a Cochrane meta-analysis [7] found limited evidence that programmes that included components for increasing cognitive and behavioural skills and avoiding relapse were more effective than programmes of the same length or shorter without these components. It even found no effect of manipulating the social interactions between participants in a group programme on outcome [7].

Taking into account all of these studies, the following conclusions can be drawn: 1) group counselling is effective for smoking cessation, 2) the inclusion of social support in a group intervention and the types of cognitive and behavioural component that are included in the group do not influence its efficacy, and 3) there is no evidence that group counselling is more effective than individual counselling.

Table 1. – Content of group treatment

Preparation session	
Timing	1 week before quit date
Duration	~2 h
Objectives	Meeting all of the other members of the group Provision of information about the treatment
	Setting of a quit date
	Advise on preparing to stop
	Explanation of withdrawal syndrome
Assessments	Level of tobacco dependence
	CO levels in expired air
Quit date session	
Timing	~1 day after quit date
Duration	~1.5–2.0 h
Objectives	Explanation of the importance of complete abstinence
	Discussion of medication issues
	Advise on coping skills
	Provision of social support (buddies)
Assessments	CO levels in expired air
Post-quit sessions	
Timing	5–12 times after quit date
Duration	~1.0–1.5 h
Objectives	Discussion of how the previous time went
	Checking medication use
	Checking withdrawal syndrome
	Discussion of issues for the next period
Assessments	CO levels in expired air
End-of-treatment session	
Timing	10–12 weeks after quit date.
Duration	~2 h
Objectives	Discussion of potential relapse situations
	Advise on coping with potential relapse situations
	Discussion of ongoing social support

Telephone counselling

Telephone counselling may have the potential to supplement face-to-face interventions or substitute for face-to-face contact as an adjunct to self-help interventions. It can also be timed to maximise the level of support around a planned quit date and can be scheduled in response to the needs of the recipient. Telephone counselling can be proactive or reactive. In the proactive approach, the counsellor initiates the calls in order to provide the smoker with support in making an attempt at quitting. Reactive counselling is provided *via* helplines or hotlines that take calls from smokers [10].

It has been found that adding proactive telephone counselling to a minimal intervention, compared with minimal intervention alone, increases long-term abstinence rates by ~50% [11]. Proactive telephone calls have some advantages over reactive calls. With proactive calls, the counsellor initiates the calls and can also increase the frequency of calls at times when the risk of relapse is at its greatest. A recent meta-analysis found that multiple call-back counselling improves long-term cessation in smokers who contact quitline services and that offering more calls may improve success rates [12].

Another means of providing telephone counselling is combination of telephone calls with a face-to-face intervention. This type of combination is indicated when the intensity of a face-to-face intervention is low or when smokers cannot attend more than a single face-to-face intervention. This can be the case for hospitalised smokers who received just one face-to-face session. In such cases, adding some support calls following discharge could be useful [12]. Nevertheless, there is no evidence to support this approach [11]. A recent meta-analysis found that younger male light smokers benefited most from telephone counselling if added to other minimal interventions [13].

Proactive telephone calls can be used in the follow-up of smokers who have received an intensive intervention for smoking cessation. Although there is no evidence that this kind of approach can reduce relapse rates, it could be recommended for the identification of those who have relapsed, and subsequently reducing the number of patients who are lost to follow-up when smoking cessation outcome is measured [14].

Telephone calls should boost the motivation of smokers to make a serious attempt at quitting, increasing their awareness about the importance of complete abstinence and facilitating the exchange of more information regarding how to deal with withdrawal symptoms.

Internet interventions

Some studies have shown that, among visitors to a smoking cessation Website, counselling letters and e-mail reminders based on psychological and addiction theory, which include advice on health risk and coping strategies, may be more effective than a shorter programme with more information concerning nicotine replacement therapy and nicotine dependence. More research is needed regarding which patients benefit and how to add Internet to other interventions [15, 16].

Behavioural therapy

Two types of behavioural therapy have been analysed: aversive smoking, and exercise therapy.

Aversion therapy pairs the pleasurable stimulus of smoking a cigarette with some unpleasant stimulus. The most frequently examined procedure is rapid smoking. Although the latest systematic Cochrane review [17] has found that rapid smoking could be effective in quitting, the single study that fulfils current criteria for methodological adequacy yields a nonsignificant trend. The results suggest that there is insufficient evidence to support the use of aversive smoking for quitting [17].

The arguments for using exercise in smoking cessation are supported by evidence that shows that exercise has a moderating effect on many of the variables negatively affected by nicotine withdrawal. There is also evidence that exercise can have a positive effect on factors that may protect against smoking relapse [17–21]. The latest systematic review [22] on the effect of exercise on smoking cessation suggests that there is insufficient evidence to support exercise for smoking cessation. It is important to note that exercise reduces weight gain following smoking cessation [22].

Complementary interventions

Hypnotherapy, acupuncture, acupressure, laser therapy and electrostimulation could be considered complementary interventions. There is no evidence that these interventions can help smokers to quit.

It can be hypothesised that hypnotherapy might be useful as an adjunct for smoking cessation for three reasons: it may weaken the desire to smoke, it may strengthen the will to stop, and it can improve the ability of the smoker to focus on a treatment programme by increasing concentration [23]. Nevertheless, according to the findings of a Cochrane systematic review [24], hypnotherapy has not been proven to have a greater effect on 6-month quit rates than other interventions or no intervention.

The rationale for using acupuncture, acupressure, electrostimulation or laser therapy as adjuncts for smoking cessation is the effects of the stimulation of the points using needle, laser or electric stimulus. These stimuli could alleviate withdrawal symptoms. Nevertheless, Cochrane systematic reviews have suggested that these interventions have no effect on smoking cessation [5, 25].

Biomedicinal risk assessments

Providing smokers with feedback regarding their biomedicinal or potential future effects of smoking, *e.g.* measurement of carbon monoxide levels in expired air, spirometry or genetic susceptibility to lung cancer, could be a possible strategy for increasing smoking cessation rates. Nevertheless, a Cochrane meta-analysis [26] did not find evidence that biomedicinal risk assessments increase smoking cessation in comparison with standard treatment.

Procedures for psychological and behavioural interventions for smoking cessation

A behavioural programme to help smokers to quit should be provided at the various clinic visits. These visits could be delivered in group or individual format. Some of the characteristics of the group format have been explained above. In this section, how to provide psychological and behavioural help to quit using an individual format is explained. This help is provided during various clinic visits: clinic visit for preparation to quit, clinic visit around quit date, and some follow-up clinic visits.

Preparation-to-quit visit

This visit lasts ~30–40 min. During the visit, the following assessments are recommended.

Smokers must be informed in detail about not only the harmful effect of smoking but also the benefits of cessation. It is important to provide personal information and to attempt to get the message across to the smoker as well as possible. Smokers must set a period after receiving this information. During this period, they should self-record their smoking in order to define their smoking pattern and determine which will be the most difficult situations. Thereafter, they should work out plans for dealing with these high-risk situations.

Smokers must choose a date on which to give up completely (quit date). They must look for a special day. They must be ready to quit completely and abruptly; the only commitment of the day must be giving up, and risk situations should be avoided, or, at least, a detailed plan should have been designed in order to manage them. Smokers should be recommended to clear all cigarettes, lighters and ashtrays out of the house, office, car and other places. Some smokers are keen on advising all of their friends that they are going to make a serious attempt at quitting in order to gain their support.

Physicians should explain the characteristics of withdrawal syndrome to smokers. Smokers should be aware that the majority of quitting smokers experience a range of different symptoms. These symptoms last 2–6 weeks and get less severe and less frequent the longer they go without a single puff. Smokers should be aware that pharmacological treatments alleviate these symptoms and know how these treatments work. Probably, one of the most frequent and severe symptoms of withdrawal syndrome is the urge to smoke. Smokers should be provided with adequate information to teach them how to cope with these urges to smoke. Table 2 shows some practical information [8].

During this visit, two important assessments should be undertaken: measurement of the level of tobacco dependence, and assessment of carbon monoxide levels in expired air. These assessments are explained in greater detail in [27].

Table 2. – Practical information for coping with urges to smoke

Evolution of urges	In the first few weeks, urges are frequent and strong; if patients do not smoke after the quit date, urges to smoke get progressively less strong and less frequent
Triggers of urges	Other people smoking or the smell of tobacco smoke Taking alcohol, coffee or other stimulants Anxiety/stress/arguments Boredom Favourite smoking places After meals New social situations
Behavioural strategies for dealing with urges	Short bursts of moderate-intensity exercise can reduce urges Keeping busy and doing something active Avoiding triggers during the first weeks of abstinence
Pharmacological strategies for dealing with urges	Use of rapid-delivery NRT system, such as chewing gum or nasal spray Regular use of NRT, varenicline or bupropion can help Taking glucose when urges arise

NRT: nicotine replacement therapy.

Quit date

It is recommended that a visit be planned for 1 day before or after the quit date. During this visit, doctors should reinforce the importance of complete abstinence and try to increase the smoker's motivation to stop. Physicians should encourage smokers to change their normal habits and put into practice all of the skills that they have learnt. Physicians should check for correct use of medication and encourage smokers to use it. This visit lasts ~10–15 min.

Follow-up

The most difficult issue in the process of quitting is to remain abstinent from smoking. A crucial part of the programme to help smokers quit is arrangement of scheduled office visits following quit day. There are different types of arrangement. Doctors must consider that the number of visits can influence the success rate: the greater the number of visits the higher the success rate. It is recommended that smokers attend the office weekly during the first month and then the number of visits be progressively diminished. The following programme can be recommended following the quite date: 1st, 2nd, 3rd, 4th, 6th, 8th, 10th, and 12th week, and 4th, 6th, and 12th month.

The following assessment should be considered for each scheduled visit.

1) The doctor must check for abstinence. Patients must be asked about their tobacco consumption and their levels of carbon monoxide in exhaled air measured. Doctors should know the real situation of the patient and be able to encourage them to continue without smoking. Smokers should see real progress in their improvement. Table 3 shows what can be done in various situations.

2) The physician must check for withdrawal syndrome. The doctor should ask about the various withdrawal symptoms and give advice on how to alleviate them or explain to the patient how the medication is working to control them. Classic withdrawal symptoms include: frequent urges to smoke, anxiety, impaired ability to concentrate, sleep disturbances, drowsiness, irritation, negative mood, increased appetite, weight

Table 3. – Suggestions for follow-up visits

If smoker is successful in complete abstinence	Congratulations Encouragement to continue Reinforcement of complete abstinence: not-even-one-puff message
If smoker has had some slips or reduced smoking	Congratulations Acknowledgement of effort made Reinforcement of complete abstinence: not-even-one-puff message Having slips makes it more difficult to overcome withdrawal symptoms Slips can easily lead to relapse and then to failure Suggestion of a new quit date for complete abstinence
If the smoker is smoking daily[#]	Acknowledgement of the effort made Advice about skills learnt Advice that new attempts will have more chance of being successful Setting of a new appointment in 6–8 months Thinking about other approaches: reduction using NRT as a step prior to quitting

NRT: nicotine replacement therapy. [#]: smokers who continue smoking daily 2–3 weeks after having received adequate treatment for their addiction should be considered unsuccessful.

gain, agitation, and restlessness. There are considerable variations in the degree to which individuals experience these symptoms, which may last for several weeks or months. The classic evolution of withdrawal shows that most symptoms are more highly intense during the first 2 weeks. Subsequently, some symptoms diminish (drowsiness, agitation, restlessness, anxiety and impaired ability to concentrate), whereas others continue (craving, increased appetite, irritation, negative mood and weight gain). Most of these symptoms almost disappear after 9–12 weeks of abstinence. Nevertheless, craving and weight gain can continue for months [28–30].

3) The doctor must check the medication, which smokers must be encouraged to take. Those who are using nicotine gum need a short period of time in order to learn how to use it correctly. The physician should explain clearly how the medication is working and for how long the medication should be used. The doctor should ask the patient about side-effects and give advice about how to avoid them. The dose should be changed if needed.

4) The following parameters should be assessed at each visit: weight, and level of carbon monoxide in expired air. Blood pressure should be measured at each visit in patients with cardiovascular diseases.

Before the end of each visit, the physician should briefly explain the highlights of the visit and encourage the patient to attend the next appointment. In general, each visit should last ~10–20 min, depending on the characteristics of the smoker.

Final follow-up visit

This visit lasts ~20–30 min. The main activity that should be undertaken during this visit is relapse prevention.

Patients should be aware that any lapse can lead to complete relapse. This happens in the majority of cases. Thus, although there is no evidence for any effective relapse prevention strategy, physicians should provide patients with information about them [14]. Several factors have been described as main causes of relapse: lack of support for cessation, weight gain, negative mood or depression, decreased motivation, strong or prolonged withdrawal syndrome, and overconfidence. [28].

Lack of support for cessation is one of the most frequent causes of relapse. Smokers should find support in different settings: healthcare professionals, family and friends, and organisations. Healthcare professionals must diagnose the characteristics of the smoker and then prescribe adequate pharmacological treatment and appropriate psychological help. Scheduled follow-up visits or telephone calls are encouraging for the patient. Smokers who make a serious attempt at quitting while receiving help from healthcare professionals multiply their chances of success [28]. Family, friends and even some social organisations can help smokers give up during the first phases of their process of quitting. Nevertheless, although some studies have indicated the positive influence of these factors, others have not [22, 31, 32].

Weight gain is the main concern regarding stopping smoking. Of all young adult females who try to quit, ~43–47% suffer from relapse due to weight gain [33]. It is crucial that healthcare professionals put this issue into focus for people trying to quit. An adequate approach to this concern is as follows: 1) clear explanation that some weight gain is common and usually self-limiting; 2) emphasis of the importance of a healthy diet but discouragement of patients from strict dieting; 3) recommendation of either starting or increasing physical activity; and 4) bupropion, 4 mg nicotine gum and rimonabant can control weight gain when used; the use of these medications can be recommended for smokers concerned about weight gain.

Depression appears in some patients who are quitting smoking. About 25% of relapses occur due to this problem [34, 35]. Those patients who have a prior history of depression or who have experienced depression during other attempts are more likely to suffer from depression in a new attempt. It is more common to suffer from negative mood than from genuine depression. These conditions usually appear between the 4th and 7th weeks of abstinence. Counselling and encouragement are usually enough to resolve them. The use of adequate medication and referral of the patient to a specialist can sometimes be required [28, 34, 35].

After 4–5 weeks of abstinence, most ex-smokers feel that they need to smoke again even more than during the first days of abstinence. This feeling is very distracting for the smoker and can lead to relapse. Smokers should be advised that such feelings are common and should be encouraged to think again of their motivation for quitting. The practice of rewarding activities during this phase can be very useful in alleviating this feeling [28].

Some smokers suffer from withdrawal syndrome for long periods, and some symptoms are very strong. Doctors must take into consideration the following aspects. 1) It is crucial to explain the evolution of the different symptoms to patients. Smokers must understand: symptoms, duration, intensity, and evolution of withdrawal syndrome. This knowledge helps maintain abstinence. 2) Doctors must consider extending the use of pharmacotherapy beyond the recommended treatment period. Prolonged use of bupropion, nicotine gum and nicotine nasal spray can be useful for these purposes [36–40]. Moreover, there is no evidence that prolonging the use of pharmacotherapy increases health risks [36, 37, 40]. 3) Physicians should consider the combination of different types of pharmacological treatment. The combined use of a system that delivers a fixed dose of nicotine with another that can self-titrate the dose is more efficacious and can control withdrawal symptoms better than the use of just one system [36, 37]. 4) Physicians should consider the use of higher doses of NRT in order to alleviate some of these strong symptoms. Increasing the nicotine dose in patches has shown some increased efficacy in diminishing the intensity of nicotine withdrawal [36, 37, 41].

Some smokers can feel confident and so relapse. Coinciding with special situations (social meetings, drinking and dining, meeting with friends, *etc.*), smokers can feel confident enough to try smoking just one cigarette. Often, this innocent cigarette can immediately lead to taking up smoking again. Doctors must clearly explain to the patient that beginning smoking, even a puff, increases urges to smoke, makes quitting more difficult and puts the patient at high risk of relapse [28].

Summary

Combining behavioural interventions with pharmacological treatment significantly increases smoking cessation success rates. Smokers who want to make a serious attempt at quitting should be encouraged to use both. Self-help programmes, brief advice, counselling, behavioural advice, biomedicinal risk assessments and other complementary interventions can be included as psychological interventions to help smokers to quit.

Self-help programmes provide no intensive contact between the therapist and the smoker. Their efficacy is low.

Brief advice provides smokers with brief information to help them quit smoking. This information should be delivered opportunistically during routine consultations with smokers whether or not they are seeking help with stopping smoking. It can be calculated that, following brief advice to 50 patients, there will be one extra quitter after 6–12 months.

Regarding the manner of providing counselling and the time consumed, there are four types of counselling: individual, group, telephone, and Internet interventions. However, all of these counselling interventions have proved to be efficacious.

Systematic reviews on the effect of exercise and aversive smoking on smoking cessation suggest that there is insufficient evidence to support these interventions for smoking cessation

Hypnotherapy, acupuncture, acupressure, laser therapy and electrostimulation could be considered complementary interventions. There is no evidence that these interventions can help smokers to quit.

A Cochrane meta-analysis did not find evidence that biomedicinal risk assessments increase smoking cessation.

A behavioural programme to help smokers to quit should be provided during various clinic visits: clinic visit for preparation to quit, clinic visit around quit date, and some follow-up clinic visits. Doctors should consider that the number of visits can influence the success rate: the greater the number of visits the higher the success rate. It is recommended that smokers attend the office weekly during the first month, and then that the number of visits diminish progressively.

Keywords: Behavioural interventions, cognitive–behavioural interventions, intensive advice, minimal advice, psychological interventions, smoking cessation.

References

1. Lancaster T, Stead LF. Self-help interventions for smoking cessation. *Cochrane Database Syst Rev* 2005; Issue 3: CD001118.
2. Lancaster T, Stead L. Physician advice for smoking cessation. *Cochrane Database Syst Rev* 2006; Issue 3: CD000165.
3. Rice V, Stead LF. Nursing interventions for smoking cessation. *Cochrane Database Syst Rev* 2005; Issue 1: CD001188.
4. McBride CM, Emmons KM, Lipkus IM. Understanding the potential of teachable moments: the case of smoking cessation. *Health Educ Res* 2003; 18: 156–170.

5. White AR, Rampes H, Ernst E. Acupuncture for smoking cessation. *Cochrane Database Syst Rev* 2002; Issue 2: CD000009.

6. Lancaster T, Stead LF. Individual behavioural counselling for smoking cessation. *Cochrane Database Syst Rev* 2002; Issue 3: CD001292.

7. Stead LF, Lancaster T. Group behaviour therapy programmes for smoking cessation. *Cochrane Database Syst Rev* 2005; Issue 2: CD001007.

8. Manual of Smoking Cessation. A Guide for Counsellors and Practitioners. Oxford, Blackwell Publishing, 2006.

9. May S, West R, Hajek P, Mcewen A, McRobbie H. Randomized controlled trial of a social support ("buddy") intervention for smoking cessation. *Patient Educ Couns* 2006; 64: 235–241.

10. Lichtenstein E.; Glasgow RE, Lando HA, Ossip-klein DJ, Boles SM. Telephone counseling for smoking cessation: rationales and meta-analytic review of evidence. *Health Educ Res* 1996; 11: 243–257.

11. Stead LF, Lancaster T, Perera R. Telephone counselling for smoking cessation. *Cochrane Database Syst Rev* 2003; Issue 1: CD002850.

12. Muller NH, Smith PM, DeBusk RF, Sobel DS, Taylor CB. Smoking cessation in hospitalised patients. Results of a randomised trial. *Arch Intern Med* 1997; 157: 409–415.

13. Pan W. Proactive telephone counseling as an adjunct to minimal intervention for smoking cessation: a meta-analysis. *Health Educ Res* 2006; 21: 416–427.

14. Hajek P, Stead LF, West R, Jarvis M, Lancaster T. Relapse prevention interventions for smoking cessation. *Cochrane Database Syst Rev* 2005; Issue 1: CD 003999.

15. Walters ST, Wrights JA, Shegog R. A review of computer and Internet-based interventions for smoking behaviour. *Addict Behav* 2006; 31: 264–277.

16. Etter JF. Comparing the efficacy of two Internet-based, computer-tailored smoking cessation programs: a randomized trial. *J Med Internet Res* 2005; 7: e2.

17. Hajek P, Stead LF. Aversive smoking for smoking cessation. *Cochrane Database Syst Rev* 2004; Issue 3: CD 000546.

18. Ussher M, Nunciata P, Cropley M, West R. Effect of a short bout of exercise on tobacco withdrawal symptoms and desire to smoke. *Psychopharmacology (Berl)* 2001; 158: 66–72.

19. Bock BC, Marcus BH, King TK, Borrelli B, Roberts MR. Exercise effects on withdrawal and mood among women attempting smoking cessation. *Addict Behav* 1999; 24: 399–410.

20. Steptoe A, Edwards S, Moses J, Mathews A. The effects of exercise training on mood and perceived coping ability in anxious adults from the general population. *J Psychosom Res* 1989; 33: 537–547.

21. McAuley E, Mihalko SL, Bane SM. Exercise and self-esteem in middle-aged adults: multi-dimensional relationships and physical fitness and self-efficacy influences. *J Behav Med* 1997; 20: 67–83.

22. Ussher MH, West R, Taylor AH, McEwen A. Exercise interventions for smoking cessation. *Cochrane Database Syst Rev* 2000; Issue 3: CD 002295.

23. Spiegel D, Frischholz EJ, Fleiss JL, Spiegel H. Predictors of smoking abstinence following a single-session restructuring intervention with self-hypnosis. *Am J Psychiatry* 1993; 150: 1090–1097.

24. Abbot NC, Stead LF, White AR, Barnes J, Ernst E. Hypnotherapy for smoking cessation. *Cochrane Database Syst Rev* 2000; Issue 2: CD001008.

25. Whites AR, Rampes H, Campbell JL. Acupuncture and related interventions for smoking cessation. *Cochrane Database Syst Rev* 2006; Issue 1: CD000009.

26. Bize R, Burnand B, Mueller Y, Cornuz J. Biomedicinal risk assessment as an aid for smoking cessation. *Cochrane Database Syst Rev* 2005; Issue 4: CD004705.

27. Fagerström KO. Assessment of the patient. *In*: Nardini S, ed. Smoking Cessation. *Eur Respir Mon* 2008; 42: 44–50.

28. Fiore MC, Bailey WC, Cohen SJ, *et al.*, Clinical Practice Guideline. Treating Tobacco Use and Dependence. Rockville, US Department of Health and Human Services, Public Health Service, 2000.

29. American Psychiatric Assocation, Diagnostic and Statistical Manual of Mental Disorders-IV. Washington, DC, American Psychiatric Association, 1994.

30. Hughes JR, Gust SW, Skoog K, Keenan RM, Fenwick JW. Symptoms of tobacco withdrawal. A replication and extension. *Arch Gen Psychiatry* 1991; 48: 52–59.

31. McIntyre-Kingsolver K, Lichtenstein E, Mermelstein RJ. Spouse training in a multicomponent smoking cessation programme. *Behav Ther* 1986; 17: 173–185.

32. Park E, Schultz JK, Tudiver F, Campbell T, Becker L. Enhancing partner support to improve smoking cessation. *Cochrane Database Syst Rev* 2004; Issue 3: CD 002928.

33. Perkins KA. Weight gain following smoking cessation. *J Consult Clin Psychol* 1993; 61: 768–777.

34. Covey L, Glassmana AH, Stetner F. Cigarette smoking and major depression. *J Addict Dis* 1998; 17: 35–46.

35. Hughes JR. Depression during tobacco abstinence. *Nicotine Tob Res* 2007; 4: 443–446.

36. Silagy C, Mant D, Fowler G, Lancaster T. Nicotine replacement therapy for smoking cessation. *Cochrane Database Syst Rev* 2000; Issue 2: CD 000146.

37. Silagy C, Lancaster T, Stead L, Mant D, Fowler G. Nicotine replacement therapy for smoking cessation. *Cochrane Database Syst Rev* 2004; Issue 3: CD000146.

38. Johnston JA, Fiedler-Kelly J, Glover ED, Pickman DE. Relationship between drug exposure and the efficacy and safety of bupropion SR for smoking cessation. *Nicotine Tob Res* 2001; 23: 744–752.

39. Durcan MJ, Deener G, White J, *et al.* The effect of bupropion SR on cigarette craving after smoking cessation. *Clin Ther* 2002; 24: 540–551.

40. Murray RP, Bailey WC, Daniels K, *et al.* Safety of nicotine polacrilex gum used by 3,094 participants in the Lung Health Study. *Chest* 1996; 109: 438–445.

41. Tonnessen P, Paoletti P, Gustavsson G, *et al.* Higher dosage nicotine patches increase one-year smoking cessation rates: results from the European CEASE-trial. *Eur Respir J* 1999; 13: 238–246.

CHAPTER 10

Pharmacological treatment for smoking cessation

C.A. Jiménez-Ruiz

Smokers' Clinic, Institute of Public Health, Madrid, Spain.

Correspondence: C.A. Jiménez-Ruiz, C/Santa Cruz del Marcenado, 9 Piso 2, 28015 Madrid, Spain. Fax: 34 912044972; E-mail: carlos.jimenez@salud.madrid.org

Smoking cessation pharmacotherapy has been extensively developed since the late 1990s. New drugs have appeared to help smokers quit, and existing medications and their doses have been adjusted to improve efficacy. In the present chapter, the neurophysiological rationale for using pharmacological treatment in those smokers who want to make a serious attempt at quitting is presented. The mechanisms of action, doses, and indications and contraindications of each one of the agents that have proved to be efficacious in helping smokers to quit are also reviewed.

Rationale for use of pharmacotherapies to treat tobacco dependence

Smokers inhale nicotine by means of consuming tobacco. Nicotine exerts its action on acetylcholinergic receptors located in neuron membranes of the ventral tegmental area of the brain. Nicotine acts on these receptors and can activate or block them more efficiently than acetylcholine. Nicotinic receptors are made up of five polypeptide chains. The most numerous nicotinic receptors are formed from two $\alpha 4$ and three $\beta 2$ chains [1, 2]. It is currently known that the stimulation of these receptors by nicotine leads to an increase in dopamine release in the nucleus accumbens. This response is what causes the reward sensation that smokers have when they use this drug and explains why it is self-administered [1, 2]. The presence of nicotine, even when many nicotinic receptors are occupied, leads to upregulation of these receptors (i.e. increases the number of receptors) and this causes dependence, tolerance and withdrawal syndrome [1]. Although, other neurophysiological pathways have been implicated in nicotine addiction, the dopaminergic pathway is the most important [1].

Conversely, it has been demonstrated that self-administration of nicotine is facilitated and enhanced when the drug supply is associated with external cues [1–4]. Furthermore, other authors have found that there are certain substances in tobacco smoke that have the property of stimulating oropharyngeal sensory receptors, which also play an important role in tobacco consumption maintenance [4, 5]. Thus external cues associated with nicotine consumption and the action of the oropharyngeal-receptor-stimulating substances also contribute to drug consumption maintenance.

Taking into account all of these considerations, it can be concluded that nicotine administration through cigarette consumption causes organic lesions in the neurons of the ventral tegmental area of the brain: increase in number and function of $\alpha 4 \beta 2$ receptors. These lesions make the smoker nicotine-dependent. Nicotine dependence

Eur Respir Mon, 2008, 42, 74–97. Printed in UK - all rights reserved. Copyright ERS Journals Ltd 2008; European Respiratory Monograph; ISSN 1025-448x.

causes physical and psychiatric alterations in the smoker (nicotine withdrawal syndrome). The presence of this syndrome is the main cause of relapse when smokers make a serious attempt at quitting. Thus the main objective of using pharmacotherapies during the smoking cessation process is to alleviate withdrawal syndrome and thus to facilitate smoking abstinence.

Three smoking cessation medications are in common use: nicotine replacement therapy (NRT), for which there are six different products, bupropion and varenicline. Other medications have been proven efficacious for smoking cessation but are used less frequently: nortriptyline, and clonidine. Others are not currently recommended for smoking cessation. Nicotine vaccine is being studied in several randomised clinical trials. In the present chapter, all of these medications are reviewed.

Nicotine replacement therapy

NRT is the most well-studied and well-documented pharmacological approach to helping smokers to quit. This treatment acts by replacing some of the nicotine smokers would have received from their cigarettes and, in doing so, reducing the severity of withdrawal syndrome. Most studies have been conducted on the safety, efficacy and mechanisms of action of this class of medication. Various forms of NRT, such as gum, patches, inhalers, nasal spray, sublingual tablets and lozenges, have been found to be efficacious and well tolerated [6].

The last meta-analysis [6] carried out demonstrated that the odds ratio (OR) for abstinence with the different types of NRT compared with the controls was 1.77 (95% confidence interval (CI) 1.66–1.88). This efficacy appears not only when the NRT is offered and controlled by a healthcare professional in the context of a smoking cessation programme but also when it is offered as an over-the-counter (OTC) product without provision of any type of psychological support [6].

Nicotine gum

Mechanism of action. Each piece of chewing gum contains 2 or 4 mg nicotine, bound to ion-exchange resin. When the gum is chewed, the nicotine is gradually released in the oral cavity. When the resin combines with the sodium and potassium ions of saliva, it is absorbed through the genian mucosa into the bloodstream. From there, it is passed to the brain, where it stimulates the nicotinic receptors of the neurons of the ventral tegmental area. When nicotine gum is used, mean blood nicotine levels of >7–10 $ng \cdot mL^{-1}$ are obtained. This value is considered the minimum needed to stimulate brain nicotinic receptors and obtain a decrease in withdrawal syndrome [7, 8].

Efficacy. The Cochrane review [6] demonstrates that the OR for abstinence using nicotine gum is 1.66 (95% CI 1.52–1.81). This efficacy is independent of the duration of therapy, intensity of psychological help that the patient receives or the context in which the cessation programme is conducted [6]. There is sufficient proof to recommend use of 4 mg (*versus* 2 mg) nicotine gum in smokers with high physical dependence (OR 2.20; 95% CI 1.85–3.25) [6].

Dosing. The chewing gum dose should be adjusted to the smoker's degree of physical dependence. The recommended dose for those who smoke <20 cigarettes·day^{-1} or who light up their first cigarette 30 min after getting up is one 2 mg piece every 1–2 h while awake. In contrast, for those who smoke ≥ 20 cigarettes·day^{-1} or who smoke their first cigarette within 30 min of awakening, 4 mg gum should be used at a similar frequency [6, 9, 10]. The treatment duration should range 8–12 weeks. In less-dependent smokers, the nicotine gum should be used for 8–10 weeks, and, when there is greater dependence, treatment should be prolonged to 3 months. However, in the latter case, it may be necessary to use the gum for up to 6–12 months. The dose should be progressively reduced after 4–8 weeks of treatment [6, 9, 10].

Contraindications and adverse events. There are some contraindications that are common to all kinds of NRT. Table 1 shows these contraindications, as well as others that are specific to each type of NRT. Denture problems and oropharyngeal infections are contraindications for using nicotine gum. Table 2 shows the most frequent adverse events for each type of NRT. Bad taste in mouth, pain in temporomandibular joint and hiccups are the most common adverse reactions for nicotine gum [6, 9–11]

Practical points. 1) Chewing gum is a relatively quick means of administering nicotine. This is one of its differential characteristics. It may be used occasionally in order to control intense craving. SHIFFMAN *et al.* [12] demonstrated that the use of nicotine gum significantly reduces the craving that can occur as a result of exposure to high-risk situations. In their study, they demonstrated that the use of chewing gum in these circumstances was effective because of not only behavioural conditioning (chewing the gum) but also the amount of nicotine supplied [12, 13].

2) Nicotine gum should be used correctly in order to achieve its greatest efficacy. The gum must be placed in the mouth and chewed slowly until the patient perceives a strong flavour. At that time, chewing should be stopped and the gum should be parked between the teeth and the buccal mucosa until the flavour has disappeared. Continuous chewing of the gum may cause the nicotine to be released too quickly so that it cannot be absorbed through the oropharyngeal mucosa. This results in the nicotine being swallowed and can cause gastric discomfort. Moreover, upon being metabolised in the liver, it would lose its therapeutic properties. In addition, it should be kept in mind that the use of acid drinks (soda, coffee, beer, *etc.*) may decrease the oral absorption of nicotine. Thus such drinks should not be drunk during or for ≥ 15 min before or after chewing.

Table 1. – Specific and common contraindications for nicotine replacement therapy

	Patch	Gum	NNS	Nicotine inhaler	Lozenge	Sublingual tablet
Specific	Severe psoriasis	Oropharyngeal infections Denture problems Lesion in temporo-mandibular joint	Rhinitis Eye infections Oropharyngeal infections	Oropharyngeal infections Bronchial hyperreactivity	Oropharyngeal infections	Oropharyngeal infections
Common						
Absolute	Myocardial infarction of <4 weeks' course Unstable angina Severe heart arrhythmias					
Relative	Pregnancy Breastfeeding Active peptic ulcer Hyperthyroidism					

NNS: nicotine nasal spray.

Table 2. – Adverse events of nicotine replacement therapy

Patch	Gum	NNS	Nicotine inhaler	Lozenge	Sublingual tablet
Local	Pain in temporo-	Rhinorrhoea	Oral/throat	Oral/throat	Oral/throat
Erythema	mandibular joint	Nasal irritation	soreness	soreness	soreness
Exanthem	Bad taste in mouth	Throat irritation		Nausea	
Eczema	Flatulence	Watery eyes			
Pruritus	Nausea	Sneezing			
Systemic	Heartburn				
Headache	Hiccups.				
Insomnia	Oral/throat soreness				
Vivid dreams					
Palpitations					
Dizziness					
Paraesthesia					
Myalgias					
Bad taste in mouth					

NNS: nicotine nasal spray.

3) Physicians should consider that learning how to use the gum takes some time. Subjects should be recommended to begin to use the gum ≥ 1 week before definitively quitting smoking. In this way, they learn how to use it correctly before quitting smoking.

4) Physicians should explain to smokers how the nicotine gum works and the differences that they can experience using gum instead of cigarettes. When smoking a cigarette, nicotine arrives at the brain in 7–10 s, but, when using a gum, the nicotine takes more time (2–3 min) to get the brain. Thus, when using gum, smokers have to wait for 2–3 min before realising the alleviation of nicotine withdrawal syndrome. Smokers should know this in order to be prepared to wait for the benefits of nicotine gum use.

5) On some occasions, nicotine gum can be used concomitantly with smoking as a means of reducing the number of cigarettes smoked daily. This approach has been proven useful for smoking cessation in smokers with special characteristics.

Nicotine patch

The patch is a nicotine-loaded device that has been prepared to deliver nicotine through the skin when applied to it

Mechanism of action. There are three types of nicotine patch on the market. They differ in the nicotine concentrations that they contain and release, release time and levels of nicotine achieved in blood. Table 3 shows the characteristics of each of them. The two patches designed for 24-h application contain and deliver higher total amounts of nicotine than the 16-h patches. Peak plasma nicotine concentrations, which are normally reached within 4–9 h after patch application, range 13–23 $ng\cdot mL^{-1}$, although levels normally range 2–11 $ng\cdot mL^{-1}$. Steady state is normally reached on the second day [14, 15].

Efficacy. A Cochrane meta-analysis [6] has demonstrated that the OR for abstinence with nicotine patches compared with placebo is 1.81 (95% CI 1.63–2.02). These values are independent of the intensity of the psychological help that the patient receives and the context in which the cessation programme is conducted. Furthermore, it has been demonstrated that 8 weeks of treatment with the patch is as effective as longer treatments, and there is not enough evidence to recommend a progressive decrease in the dose *versus* abrupt cessation [6, 16]. The 24-h patches are as effective as the 16-h ones [6].

Table 3. – Types of nicotine patch

	Novartis	Johnson & Johnson	GlaxoSmithKline
Application time h	24	16	24
Size cm^2	30	30	21
	20	20	15
	10	10	7
Nicotine content mg	52.5	24	114
	35	16.6	78
	17.5	8.3	36
Nicotine absorbed mg	21	15	20.6
	14	10	14
	7	5	7

Dosing. The patches should be used for a period of 8–12 weeks. During the first 4–6 weeks, patches should be used at high doses. In the case of 16-h patches, the recommended dose is 15 mg·day^{-1} for 4–6 weeks and then 10 mg·day^{-1} for 4 weeks followed by 5 mg·day^{-1} for a further 2 weeks. The recommended dose for the 24-h nicotine patch is 21 mg·day^{-1} for 4–6 weeks and then 14 mg·day^{-1} for 4 weeks followed by 7 mg·day^{-1} for a further 2–4 weeks. Nevertheless, it should be taken into consideration that, using these doses, only 35–40% nicotine replacement is obtained. Thus some authors recommend adjusting doses to the number of cigarettes smoked daily. For the 24-h nicotine patch, a dose of 42 mg·day^{-1} is recommended in those who smoked >40 cigarettes·day^{-1}. In those who smoked 21–39 cigarettes·day^{-1}, doses of 28–35 mg·day^{-1} are recommended. When the number of cigarettes smoked daily is 10–20, doses of 14–21 mg·day^{-1} are recommended, and, finally, in those who smoked <10 cigarettes·day^{-1}, the recommended dose is 14 mg·day^{-1} [6, 9–11, 17, 18]. For the 16-h nicotine patch, a dose of 25 mg·day^{-1} is recommended in those who smoked >20 cigarettes·day^{-1}, and, in those who smoked ≤20 cigarettes·day^{-1}, the starting dose is 15 mg·day^{-1} [6, 9–11, 16].

Contraindications and adverse events. Table 1 shows the contraindications for using nicotine patches. Table 2 shows the most frequent adverse events when using this kind of NRT. Skin reactions and pruritus occur most frequently. Nevertheless, this is one of the safest means of administering nicotine [6, 9–11].

Practical points. 1) The patch should be applied on a hairless clean area of the skin, on the upper limbs or trunk. The patch should be applied every day when the subject gets up and be removed at bedtime on the same day if the patch is for 16 h, or on the next day, after getting up, if the patch is for 24 h of release. This is an ideal replacement treatment and does not require very active collaboration from the smoker. This characteristic, together with the ease of use and limited adverse effects produced, makes it one of the most-used forms of NRT on the OTC market.

2) Local skin reactions and itching are the more frequent adverse reactions. Rotating the site where the patch is applied and waving the patch in the air before it is placed are two recommendations for avoiding some of these adverse reactions.

3) It is recommended that the dose be adjusted to the number of cigarettes smoked daily. In those smokers who wake up in the night to smoke, the use of 24-h nicotine patches is recommended. Sometimes, 24-h nicotine patches produce nightmares or other dream disturbances. In such cases, it is recommended that the patch be taken off before going bed or a change be made to 16-h nicotine patches.

Nicotine nasal spray

Nicotine nasal spray (NNS) delivers nicotine through the lining of the nose when sprayed directly into each nostril.

Mechanism of action. This device delivers nicotine faster than other therapeutic NRT delivery systems. It takes <10 min to reach maximum concentrations. When it is used regularly, nicotine concentrations after 12 h range 13–18 $ng \cdot mL^{-1}$, depending on the dose applied [19].

Efficacy. The Cochrane meta-analysis [6] demonstrated that the OR for abstinence with nicotine spray compared with placebo was 2.35 (95% CI 1.63–3.38). These values are independent of the intensity of the psychological help that the patient receives and of the context in which the cessation programme is conducted.

Dosing. A dose consists of 1 mg, 0.5 mg to each nostril. The recommended dosing is 1–2 $doses \cdot h^{-1}$, but not exceeding 3 $doses \cdot h^{-1}$ or 40 $doses \cdot day^{-1}$. Each spray contains 0.5 mg nicotine.

Contraindications and adverse events. Table 1 shows contraindications for NNS. Table 2 shows the most frequently occurring adverse events when using this kind of NRT. Rhinorrhoea, nasal and throat irritation, and watery eyes are the most common adverse reactions [6, 9–11]. All of these reactions decrease after 1 week of use. Since it is a rapid nicotine delivery device, there was concern that NNS could have long-term abuse liability. Nevertheless, some information has confirmed that the potential for abuse is low [20, 21].

Practical points. 1) The main advantage of this device is its faster delivery of nicotine compared with other NRTs. For this reason, it is able to control stress and the urge to smoke better than nicotine gum.

2) Patients should be aware of the adverse reactions that can appear during the first week of use. Approximately 90% of users suffer from nose and eye irritation during the first week of treatment, and this can lead patients to abandon NNS. Smokers should be advised that these adverse events last 5–7 days and then disappear.

3) NNS shouldn't be sniffed into the nose. Rather, it should be sprayed against the lining of each nostril. Otherwise it causes more adverse events.

Nicotine inhaler

This device is a plastic holder into which a cartridge containing a cotton plug impregnated with 10 mg nicotine plus 10% menthol is inserted. It delivers a nicotine vapour that is absorbed through the oral mucosa. Menthol masks the nicotine taste and reduces irritation.

Mechanism of action. When the smoker sucks through the device, they obtain ~0.1 µM nicotine in blood. (Having a puff on a cigarette gives 1 µM.) The concentrations of nicotine depend upon air temperature. With higher ambient temperature, the concentrations of nicotine increase. Nevertheless, none of the nicotine reaches the pulmonary alveoli, even with deep inhalation. Most of the nicotine is deposited buccally or in the upper respiratory tract [22]. For this reason, the nicotine inhaler does not provide high arterial nicotine levels. The inhaler results in approximately the same nicotine concentration as 2 mg gum.

Efficacy. *A* Cochrane meta-analysis [6] has demonstrated that the OR for abstinence with a nicotine inhaler compared with placebo is 2.14 (95% CI 1.44–3.18). These values are independent of the intensity of the psychological help that the patient receives and the context in which the cessation programme is conducted.

Dosing. The recommended initial dose of the nicotine inhaler is 6–16 cartridges·day^{-1}. The optimal treatment duration is 12 weeks, with the last 4–6 weeks utilised for tapering [6]. Each cartridge is designed for 80 puffs over 20 min of use. Achieving effect is independent of inhalation. Patients do not need to inhale deeply to achieve an effect [22].

Contraindications and adverse events. Table 1 shows contraindications for the nicotine inhaler. Table 2 shows the most frequent adverse events when using this kind of NRT. It is a very safe delivery system. It can cause mouth and throat irritation [6, 9–11].

Practical points. 1) This device mimics the hand-to-mouth behaviour of smoking. For some smokers, this may be a useful adjunct, but, for others, may act as a smoking cue that could undermine cessation.
   2) It is recommended that the device be warmed by holding it in the fist before sucking it.
   3) In order to increase efficacy, it is recommended that >6 cartridges·day^{-1} be used.

Nicotine lozenge

The nicotine lozenge is available in 2- and 4-mg doses. It delivers nicotine through the lining of the mouth while the lozenge dissolves. A 1-mg lozenge is available in some countries.

Mechanism of action. The amount of nicotine absorbed per lozenge is greater than that delivered by the gum, giving 8–10% higher maximum plasma concentrations and 25–27% higher areas under the curve from 2- and 4-mg lozenges compared to gum at both the 2- and 4-mg dose levels [23].

Efficacy. There is only one trial reporting the efficacy of this NRT. In this trial, smokers were allocated to the 2- or 4-mg group depending upon the time to their first cigarette. After 1 yr, the success rate in the highly dependent group (those who smoked within 30 min of waking) was 6% on placebo and 15% on 4-mg lozenges. For the less dependent (those who smoked after 30 min), the success rates were 10% on placebo and 18% on 2-mg lozenges [24].

Dosing. The indication for the lozenges allocates smokers to the 2- or 4-mg dose based on how soon after waking the first cigarette of the day is smoked. Those who smoke within 30 min should use 4-mg lozenges and those who smoke after 30 min should use 2-mg lozenges [24]. Based on daily cigarette consumption, 4-mg lozenges can be recommended for those who smoke >20 cigarettes·day^{-1}, 2-mg lozenges for those who smoke 11–20 cigarettes·day^{-1} and 1-mg lozenges for those who smoke ≤10 cigarettes·day^{-1}. Initial dosing is one or two lozenges every 1–2 h for a minimum of 9 days. Tapering is recommended for 8–10 weeks.

Contraindications and adverse events. Table 1 shows contraindications for nicotine lozenges. Table 2 shows the most frequent adverse events when using this kind of NRT. Nausea is a frequent adverse event [24].

Practical points. 1) There are two advantages of the lozenges compared to the gum: chewing is not required, and the amount of nicotine absorbed per lozenge appears to be greater than that delivered by gum (25% greater) [23].

2) Dosing should be adjusted according to the number of cigarettes smoked daily or the time to first cigarette of the day. Smokers should not eat or drink during or for ≥ 15 min before use.

3) Lozenges should not be chewed or swallowed.

Sublingual nicotine tablets

These tablets contain 2 mg nicotine. Subjects should put them under their tongue; they are diluted in $\sim$15–20 min. The recommended dose of this medication is dependent upon baseline cigarette consumption. Subjects who smoked ≥ 16 cigarettes·day^{-1} should use 1–2 tablets·h^{-1} (minimum 10 tablets·day^{-1} and maximum 40 tablets·day^{-1}); those smoking 10–15 cigarettes·day^{-1} should use 1 tablet·h^{-1} (6–30 tablets·day^{-1}); and those smoking 6–9 cigarettes·day^{-1} should use 1 tablet·h^{-1} (3–10 tablets·day^{-1}); a dose of 40 tablets·day^{-1} should not be exceeded. It is recommended that smokers use the product for ≥ 12 weeks and that the dose be tapered after that time [25, 26].

Combining nicotine replacement therapy

The combination of two types of NRT with different types of delivery, one rapid (generally the gum) to achieve a more effective control of craving, and the other slow (generally the patch) to achieve improvement in abstinence syndrome symptoms, is a NRT regimen that has been tested in several studies [27–29]. It has been demonstrated for all of them that the use of combined therapy is more effective than use of each therapy separately (OR 1.9; 95% CI 1.3–2.6) [6, 27–29]. It is important to indicate here that this increase in efficacy obtained with combined therapy is due more to the combination of two administration forms of nicotine (rapid and slow simultaneously) than to the administration of greater amounts of nicotine [30].

The patch should be used at doses as described above; 2-mg gum, 2-mg lozenge, nicotine inhaler or NNS should be prescribed for when acute withdrawal symptoms and urges to use tobacco occur. Sometimes, when acute forms of NRT are used frequently, it is necessary to adjust the patch dose. The goal is to minimise need for short-acting NRT devices.

This treatment should be considered for those who are highly dependent or who have failed using monotherapy [6, 27–30].

Use of nicotine replacement therapy in smokers with pulmonary diseases

Pulmonary patients who smoke can suffer from a higher degree of nicotine dependence than healthy smokers. Moreover, most of them exhibit anxiety, panic disorder and even depression. This comorbid condition could worsen the efficacy of smoking cessation treatments in these patients [31–33].

The efficacy of NRT in smokers with chronic obstructive pulmonary disease (COPD) has been analysed in several clinical trials [26, 34, 35]. The Lung Health Study was a multicentric randomised controlled trial designed to determine whether or not a programme incorporating a smoking cessation intervention and regular use of an inhaled bronchodilator in smokers at high risk of COPD can slow the annual decline in lung function (forced expiratory volume in one second).The results showed that, after 12 months, nicotine gum in combination with an intensive behavioural programme was significantly more effective at helping smokers at risk of COPD to abstain from smoking than usual care [34]. Nevertheless, it should be mentioned that this study made no attempt to compare NRT *versus* placebo. The efficacy of NRT could be confounded by the fact that the subjects who received NRT also received extensive counselling support.

Nevertheless, the first randomised controlled trial demonstrating the efficacy of NRT for smoking cessation in patients with COPD has been undertaken using sublingual nicotine tablets. The trial enrolled 370 COPD smokers who were treated with this medication at adequate doses (see above) or placebo for 12 weeks. This trial also evaluated the efficacy of low and high support. It had a two-by-two design, with four treatment groups: sublingual nicotine tablet plus low support, sublingual nicotine tablet plus high support, placebo sublingual tablet plus low support, and placebo sublingual tablet plus high support. Smoking cessation rates were significantly superior in the active treatment group compared with the placebo group at both the 6- and 12-month follow-up (23 *versus* 10% and 17 *versus* 10%, respectively). There was no significant difference in effect between low and high provision of support [26].

Taking into account these considerations, it should be considered that NRT at high doses and the combination of different forms of NRT could be more efficacious in these patients. Patients who have been treated with NRT in a previous attempt and been unsuccessful should be considered for these approaches in a new attempt to quit. In such cases, the use of NRT can be prolonged for up to 6–12 months.

Pulmonary patients who smoke and are unable to set a quit date or do not want to quit should be recommended to use NRT (nicotine gum or nicotine inhaler) to help them to progressively reduce their smoking in a reduction-to-quit approach. This method can help them to build up their self-efficacy in quitting and to increase their motivation to set a quit date [10, 36].

Use of nicotine replacement therapy in pregnant and breastfeeding subjects

Several studies have been carried out evaluating the risk of using NRT in pregnant subjects. These studies have concluded that the risks associated with smoking during pregnancy are significantly greater than those associated with pure nicotine use. However, the use of NRT during pregnancy has not been shown to be totally innocuous for the foetus and mother. Hence an adequate evaluation of the risk/benefit ratio should be undertaken before recommending use of NRT in pregnant females [9, 37–43]. Before drug treatment is initiated, the physician and patient should together perform a joint analysis regarding whether or not the increase in the possibility of quitting smoking due to this treatment and the benefits associated with giving up smoking are greater than the health risks that the mother and foetus may experience as a consequence of using this type of treatment. Once it has been established that drug treatment is needed, this should be prescribed as soon as possible, and always in combination with psychosocial treatment. It is preferable to use the *ad libitum* forms; nicotine chewing gum is better than patches. However, the type of NRT to be used should be individualised. Use of patches rather than chewing gum is preferable in those subjects whose pregnancy is accompanied by frequent vomiting and nausea. When nicotine patch use has been established, it is best to prescribe 16- rather than 24-h patches. Dosing should be halved [9, 37–43].

The risk exists that certain amounts of nicotine ingested by a nursing female who is using a form of NRT may be eliminated through the milk [1]. Thus use of NRT in nursing subjects should be adapted using the same considerations as in pregnant ones [9, 37–43].

Bupropion

Bupropion is a white powder with a bitter taste that is provided in sustained-release (SR)-tablet form and contains 150 mg active ingredient. It was the first non-nicotine medication to be licensed for smoking cessation [9].

Mechanism of action

The action mechanism of this drug is incompletely known. It is presumed that it acts on the nucleus accumbens, inhibiting neuronal reuptake of dopamine. This effect would explain the reduction in craving experienced by smokers who take it. It also inhibits neuronal reuptake of noradrenalin in the nucleus ceruleus, thus achieving a significant reduction in the intensity of nicotine withdrawal syndrome [44]. Recent *in vitro* studies have detected that bupropion is a noncompetitive functional inhibitor of nicotinic acetylcholine receptors. This anti-nicotinic activity may contribute to its efficacy in the treatment of nicotinic dependence [45].

Efficacy

The last meta-analysis [46] analysed 40 trials in which bupropion was used as pharmacotherapy for smoking cessation. In 31 trials, bupropion was used as the sole pharmacotherapy and was found to double the odds of cessation (OR 1.94; 95% CI 1.72–2.19). Three trials analysed the efficacy of extended therapy with bupropion to prevent relapse after initial cessation but did not find evidence of a significant long-term benefit. From the available data, bupropion appears to be equally effective and of similar efficacy to NRT. Pooling three trials comparing bupropion to varenicline showed a lower odds of quitting with bupropion (OR 0.60; 95% CI 0.46–0.78) [46]. Although smoking abstinence rates were higher with combination therapy (NRT plus bupropion) than with bupropion alone, the differences were nonsignificant. Currently, there is insufficient evidence that adding bupropion to NRT provides an additional long-term benefit [46–48].

Recently, a study analysed pooled data from two clinical trials of bupropion for smoking cessation for which data on the D_2 dopamine receptor gene (*DRD2*) Taq1A genotype were available. A total of 722 smokers across the two trials were randomised to 10 weeks of bupropion hydrochloride SR or placebo. The authors found that smokers with the A2/A2 genotype using bupropion were more then three times as likely, relative to placebo, to be abstinent at end of treatment (35.2 *versus* 15.1%; OR 3.25; 95% CI 2.00–5.28) and at 6 months of follow-up (26.7 *versus* 12.2%; OR 2.81; 95% CI 1.66–4.77), which was attenuated by 12 months (16.3 *versus* 10.7%; OR 1.70; 95% CI 0.95–3.05). Nevertheless, the authors did not find a significant benefit of bupropion relative to placebo on smoking cessation outcomes at any time-point in participants with the A1/A1 or A1/A2 genotype. These data suggest that bupropion may be effective for smoking cessation only in the subgroup of smokers with the *DRD2* Taq1 A2/A2 genotype [49]. Nevertheless, further studies are needed.

Dosing

Bupropion should be used for a period of 9–12 weeks at a dosage of 300 mg daily, taken in two doses of 150 mg each. Treatment should be initiated 7 days before the targeted quit date. During the first 7 days, the subject should only take one 150-mg tablet daily, and, after this period, increase the dose to two 150-mg tablets coinciding with the targeted quit date. Doses must be taken ≥ 8 h apart. The dose should be halved in smokers aged ≥ 65 yrs or those who show significant kidney or liver failure or low weight (<45 kg) [50].

Adverse events

Bupropion is generally well tolerated. The most common adverse events associated with bupropion SR treatment for smoking cessation are dry mouth, insomnia, headache and cutaneous rash. They were reported approximately twice as frequently with bupropion SR as with placebo in controlled clinical trials. The most medically important serious adverse event reported with bupropion is seizure, which occurs infrequently (1:1,000) and is associated with risk factors such as the presence of a seizure disorder (*e.g.* epilepsy), significant head trauma or brain injury, an eating disorder (*e.g.* bulimia or anorexia nervosa) and concurrent medications that lower the seizure threshold. There is also a small risk of severe allergic reactions [50, 51].

Contraindications

Table 4 shows the main contraindications for using bupropion and the situations in which bupropion should be used with caution. In such cases, it is recommended that a risk/benefit assessment be undertaken before prescribing bupropion [50, 51].

Practical points

1) Insomnia is one of the most frequent adverse events caused by bupropion. There is a dose–response relationship. Reduction of the dose to 150 mg daily is recommended in

Table 4. – Contraindications and precautions when using bupropion

Precautions	Contraindications
Use of medications lowering seizure threshold	Smokers aged <18 yrs
Antidepressants	Pregnant subjects
Antipsychotics	Hypersensitivity to bupropion.
Antimalarials	Current or previous seizure disorder
Others	Current or previous diagnosis of bulimia or anorexia
Current use of stimulants and anorectics	nervosa
Alcohol abuse	Tumour of central nervous system
History of head injury	Withdrawal from alcohol or benzodiazepines
Use of medications metabolised by isoenzyme CYP2B6	History of bipolar disorder
Cimetidine	Severe hepatic cirrhosis
Sodium valproate	Concomitant use of monoamine oxidase inhibitors
Cyclophosphamide	
Use of medications metabolised by isoenzyme CYP2D6	
Type 1C antiarrhythmics	
β-Blockers	

CYP2B6: cytochrome P_{450}, family 2, subfamily B, polypeptide 6; CYP2D6: cytochrome P_{450}, family 2, subfamily D, polypeptide 6.

those suffering from this adverse reaction. Moreover, when the results of different clinical trials were pooled, there was no added advantage in 1-yr abstinence rates between 300 and 150 mg·day^{-1} [46].

2) Under certain circumstances, bupropion is combined with NRT. In such cases, it is recommended that periodic blood pressure measurements be taken since treatment-emergent hypertension can occur during this therapy [47].

3) Bupropion can be used in those smokers who are concerned about weight gain after quitting smoking. Various studies have found that bupropion can control the weight gain associated with smoking cessation better than placebo [46]. HAYS et al. [52] found that, after 1 yr of treatment with bupropion, there was significantly less weight gain in the active group than in the placebo group. This difference remained 1 yr after bupropion was discontinued.

4) There is no drug–drug interaction to preclude the use of bupropion with either selective serotonin reuptake inhibitors or tricyclic antidepressants.

Use of bupropion in smokers with pulmonary diseases

There are very few studies utilising bupropion for smoking cessation treatments in subjects with pulmonary diseases. The most recent study compared the efficacy of bupropion with placebo and nortriptyline in smokers with or at risk of COPD. It found that bupropion was more effective than placebo for achieving continuous abstinence at 6 months of follow-up in COPD (27.9 versus 14.6% in the COPD smoker group), but not in the group at risk of COPD [53].

Another study by TASHKIN et al. [54] examined the effectiveness of bupropion on smoking cessation among patients with COPD. Compared to placebo, bupropion nearly doubled the 6-month point prevalence (23 versus 16%) and significantly increased continuous smoking abstinence rates (16 versus 9%) among those with mild-to-moderate COPD [54].

Although GARCIA-RIO et al. [55] have hypothesised that bupropion could depress the ventilatory responses to hypoxaemia and hypercapnia of carotid body chemoreception and that this could have a potentially harmful effect in patients with COPD, none of these studies found an increase in the number or intensity of adverse effects associated with taking bupropion [53–55].

It is important to consider that none of these studies have presented results at 12 months of follow-up. More studies are required focusing on the long-term efficacy and safety of bupropion in smokers with pulmonary disorders.

Varenicline

Varenicline is the first drug specifically developed to aid smokers quitting smoking. It has recently been approved as a specific treatment for smoking cessation in the USA and Europe.

Mechanism of action

Varenicline acts as a selective partial agonist for the nicotinic receptor of the neurons of the ventral tegmental area of the brain. As it is a partial agonist, it shows common characteristics of both agonists and antagonists. As it is an agonist, it is capable of stimulating the nicotinic receptor and thus of controlling craving and withdrawal syndrome. However, as it is an antagonist, it can block the effect of nicotine on the receptor. Thus, due to the use of vareniciline in a smoker who is quitting, the relapses that the smoker may suffer are not accompanied by a pleasant and rewarding sensation. Thus this drug helps to prevent a relapse from becoming a failure [56, 57].

Efficacy

A meta-analysis [58] reviewed four clinical trials that studied the efficacy of varenicline and found that this drug was significantly more effective than placebo for achieving continuous abstinence at not only the end of the treatment (OR 3.75; 95% CI 2.65–5.30) but also the end of 1 yr of follow-up (OR 2.96; 95% CI 2.12–4.12). In this same study, three clinical trials that evaluated the efficacy of varenicline *versus* bupropion were analysed. It was found that varenicline was more effective than bupropion at not only the end of the treatment (OR 1.61; 95% CI 1.16–2.21) but also the end of 1 yr of follow-up (OR 1.58; 95% CI 1.22–2.05) [59–63]. More recently, clinical trials conducted in Japanese and Asian populations have confirmed the efficacy and safety of this treatment in these groups [64, 65].

Some analyses have been undertaken in order to evaluate the efficacy of varenicline according to the level of baseline nicotine dependency as measured by Fagerström Test for Nicotine Dependence questionnaire. The results of these analyses suggest that higher levels of nicotine dependency result in lower continuous abstinence rates, as occurs with other treatment options [66].

At the current moment, there is no randomised placebo-controlled study comparing the efficacy and safety of varenicline *versus* NRT. The only published study is an open before/after comparison between varenicline and NRT. The results showed that short-term cessation rates (4 weeks after quit date) were higher with varenicline than with NRT (OR 1.70; 95% CI 1.09–2.67). Moreover, there was a significantly higher incidence of nausea, disturbed sleep, drowsiness, constipation, headache, dyspepsia, dry mouth, bad taste, low mood, diarrhoea and disorientation in those taking varenicline [67]. This is a preliminary study and many controlled and long-term follow-up studies are required in order to confirm these results.

Dosing

It has been established that varenicline at a dose of 1 mg twice daily for 12 weeks is effective and safe as a tobacco dependence treatment. During the first week, the subject may smoke and should use a 0.5-mg dose of the drug once daily for the first 3 days and then twice daily until completion of the first week. After this time, the subject should stop smoking and begin to use a 1-mg dose of the drug twice daily until completion of 12 weeks of treatment [59, 60].

To date, two studies have been carried out in which long-term treatment with varenicline was used [68, 69]. One of them showed that the prolongation of the use of varenicline until completion of 24 weeks of treatment could produce a significant increase in continuous abstinence rates compared to placebo at both 6 and 12 months of follow-up. The results were as follows: 70.6 *versus* 49.6% (OR 2.48; 95% CI 1.95–3.16) at 6 months, and 43.6 *versus* 36.9% (OR 1.34; 95% CI 1.06–1.69) at 12 months. An important fact is that increased treatment time did not increase adverse effects [68]. Another study analysed varenicline safety at the usual doses *versus* placebo, but with 12 months' continuous use. The study included a total of 251 smokers in the active group *versus* 126 in the placebo one. The results showed that no greater intensity of adverse effects nor new appearances were detected. Moreover, it was observed that the point prevalence abstinence rate was never less than 35.1% and reached 49% at 8 weeks of treatment. The differences with regard to placebo were significant at all times [69].

Adverse events and contraindications

Table 5 shows the main adverse events that have appeared in the various clinical trials. Nausea is the most frequent one and generally appears during the first week of treatment. It is mild in >70% of cases and does not necessitate discontinuation of treatment. The nausea is usually self-limiting over time and does not require treatment [56, 57, 59–62, 64, 65, 68]. The use of varenicline for 12 months produces the following adverse events: nausea (40 versus 7.9%), abnormal dreams (22.7 versus 7.0%), and insomnia (19 versus 9.5%) [69].

Recently, the manufacturer, in collaboration with the US Food and Drug Administration (FDA), has taken into consideration some adverse events that have appeared during post-marketing experience with varenicline: depressed mood, agitation, changes in behaviour, suicidal ideation, and suicide. These events were reported voluntarily by patients attempting to quit smoking while taking varenicline. Since these events were reported voluntarily by a population of uncertain size, it is not always possible to reliably establish a causal relationship to the drug [70]. Moreover, some studies have found that smoking cessation, with or without treatment, is associated with the exacerbation of underlying psychiatric illness [71]. The most recent clinical study focusing on the safety of varenicline in those with mental illness found that there was no evidence that adverse symptoms were experienced more in those with mental illness than in healthy smokers, or that, when experienced, the symptoms were more severe [67]. Thus there is no scientific evidence establishing a causal relationship between varenicline and these adverse events. The FDA and European Agency for the Evaluation of Medicinal Products are working closely with the manufacturer to review these post-marketing reports. Until further insight is obtained, smokers using varenicline should be advised by their doctors of these events [70].

Practical points

1) Nausea is the most frequent adverse event. In order to manage it adequately, it is important to know that it is usually self-limiting over a period of 1 week and can be avoided by taking the medication with food and resting for a while after taking it.

2) Varenicline use for 12 weeks is effective. Nevertheless, if not smoking at the end of this time, continuation at 1 mg twice daily for an additional 12 weeks could be considered [68, 72].

3) More and better-designed studies are required in order to establish the efficacy and safety of varenicline versus NRT [67].

4) A systematic review [58] found that, compared with bupropion, varenicline increased the odds of smoking cessation ~1.7 fold at 1 yr, although this result was based on studies that have received industry funding [58, 73].

5) There is a lack of clinical trials demonstrating the efficacy and safety of varenicline when prescribed by general practitioners with routine brief advice.

Table 5. – Adverse events of varenicline

Nausea	28
Flatulence	2–5
Insomnia	13–15
Abnormal dreams	11–13

Data are presented as percentages.

6) Some randomised clinical studies investigating the efficacy and safety of varenicline in smokers with COPD and smokers with cardiovascular disorders are currently ongoing. Their results must be awaited before use of this medication in smokers with these disorders is considered.

Nortriptyline

Nortriptyline is a tricyclic antidepressant that inhibits the reuptake of noradrenalin and serotonin. It is considered a second-line medication for smoking cessation in US smoking cessation guidelines [9]. There are several randomised clinical trials that have shown a significant effect with active nortriptyline compared with a placebo [74, 75]. The most recent meta-analysis [46] identified four trials using this drug. The results revealed an OR of 2.34 (95% CI 1.61–3.40). Nortriptyline has been used at doses of 75–100 mg·day^{-1}, with a duration of treatment of 8–12 weeks. The dose should be started at 25 mg·day^{-1} and increased gradually over a period of 3 weeks to the target dose of 75–100 mg·day^{-1}. The quit date should be set when the therapeutic level has been reached (~10–30 days after starting medication). After 12 weeks of treatment, the dose should be tapered. Nortriptyline in combination with transdermal nicotine was also shown to enhance cessation rates above levels seen with transdermal nicotine alone [76].

Although, nortriptyline has the potential for serious side-effects (cardiovascular effects), none of them have been seen in the few small trials for smoking cessation. The most common adverse effects that appeared in these trials were as follows: sedation, dry mouth, blurred vision, urinary retention, constipation, and low blood pressure on standing.

Contraindications for the use of this medication are as follows: arrhythmia, myocardial infarction, and severe hepatic insufficiency. It must be taken with caution in patients with a history of epilepsy, cardiac disease or psychosis or in those who are pregnant or breastfeeding.

Clonidine

Clonidine is an imidazoline that has been reported to show limited efficacy as a smoking cessation therapy [77]. It has been recommended as a second-line therapy in US smoking cessation guidelines [9]. Clonidine can suppress the acute symptoms of nicotine withdrawal. It can be taken orally or through a transdermal patch. When given orally, the recommended dose of clonidine for smoking cessation is 100 µg twice daily, but it can be titrated to a maximum of ~400 µg·day^{-1} according to tolerance. Treatment should start before stopping smoking so that steady-state plasma concentrations can be achieved before the onset of nicotine withdrawal symptoms. Transdermal doses range 0.1–0.3 mg·day^{-1}. The maximum duration of treatment should not exceed 3–4 weeks. However, adverse effects associated with clonidine, such as drowsiness, fatigue and dry mouth, may limit its use.

A Cochrane review [77] identified 21 studies focusing on the efficacy of clonidine for smoking cessation. Only six studies met the inclusion criteria, and the pooled results showed an OR of 1.89 (95% CI 1.30–2.74) [77].

Some situations in which the use of clonidine may be considered appropriate include those cases in which NRT, bupropion, varenicline or nortriptyline have failed in the presence of multiple drug abuse problems; this is because clonidine relieves the withdrawal symptoms of drugs other than nicotine. Physicians should be aware of the presence of side-effects.

Antidepressants

Antidepressants other than nortriptyline and bupropion have been used for smoking cessation. The use of antidepressants as pharmacological treatment for smoking cessation is based on different mechanisms of action: improvement of withdrawal symptoms, nicotine receptor antagonism, and substitution for possible antidepressant effects of nicotine. Nevertheless, none of them have been proven [46, 71]. Several antidepressants have been studied. Selective serotonin reuptake inhibitors, such as fluoxetine, sertraline, and paroxetine, have been proven not to show significant benefit in terms of increasing smoking cessation rates in various trials. None of them detected significant long-term effects, and there was no evidence of a significant benefit when results were pooled [46]. Doxepin and imipramine failed to show an effect in two different small short-term follow-up trials [46]. Other trials have investigated venlafaxine and tryptophan; neither found any beneficial effect [46].

Mecamylamine

Mecamylamine is a nicotine antagonist. The rationale for its use in smoking cessation is that it may block the rewarding effect of nicotine and thus reduce the urge to smoke. It has been found to be more effective when combined with NRT.

In 2000, a Cochrane review [78] identified two studies on this subject, both from the same investigators. Data from these two small studies suggested that the combination of nicotine and mecamylamine could be superior to nicotine alone in promoting smoking cessation. The authors concluded that the results required confirmation in larger studies before the treatment could be recommended clinically [78]. A new larger study using a combination of mecamylamine and nicotine patches has recently been published. It was a multicentric double-blind randomised parallel-group repeat-dose study. A total of 540 subjects were enrolled, 180 patients in each of the three treatment arms: one group received patches with 21 mg nicotine plus 6 mg mecamylamine, another group received patches with 21 mg nicotine plus 3 mg mecamylamine, and the other group received patches with 21 mg nicotine plus 0 mg mecamylamine. Analysis of the 4-week continuous abstinence for the intent-to-treat population showed overall rates of 29, 29 and 23 in each group, respectively. The authors concluded that addition of mecamylamine to NRT does not significantly increase the chances of success at stopping smoking [79].

Monoamine oxidase inhibitors

Monoamine oxidase inhibitors may aid smoking cessation through their ability to inhibit dopamine metabolism. Selegiline, lazabemide and moclobemide have been investigated in different trials. No systematic reviews have been undertaken with selegiline; nevertheless, three small short-term follow-up trials have proven that sergiline could alleviate withdrawal symptoms and improve outcome [80–82].

Lazabemide could produce liver toxicity and its use as a smoking cessation treatment is limited [83]. Moclobemide appeared to be effective at 6 months, but not at 12 months, of follow-up in one randomised clinical trial [84].

Anxiolytics

It is known that anxiety decreases after smoking cessation. Thus there is no rationale for using anxiolytics as a pharmacological treatment for smoking cessation [85, 86].

Buspirone, diazepam, meprobamate, ondansetrom and three β-blockers (propanolol, metoprolol and oxprenolol) have been investigated in various clinical trials. None of them have shown any benefit of using these medications [86].

Naloxone

The rationale for using opioid antagonists for smoking cessation comes from the principle that endogenous opioids could play a role in the reinforcing effects of nicotine. The longer-acting formulation of naloxone, naltrexone, has been investigated in two long-term studies. The results of both studies failed to demonstrate a significant effect at 6 months of follow-up. Even when their results were pooled, the conclusion was irrelevant (OR 1.34; 95% CI 0.49–3.63) [87].

Lobeline

Lobeline is a partial nicotine agonist that has been used as a pharmacological treatment for smoking cessation since the 1930s. A Cochrane meta-analysis [88] did not find any randomised trials comparing lobeline to placebo, or an alternative therapeutic control, that reported smoking cessation with at least 6 months of follow-up. The authors concluded that there was no evidence to suggest that lobeline is effective as a smoking cessation aid [88].

Silver acetate

The rationale for using silver acetate as a smoking cessation aid is that, when it is used in combination with smoking, an unpleasant metallic taste is produced; thus it is a form of aversion therapy for smoking cessation.

Argyria is an adverse effect that can appear if total doses exceed 756 mg. Nevertheless, the only Cochrane meta-analysis [89] that has been undertaken did not find any advantage of this medication on abstinence rates compared with placebo.

Nicobrevin

Nicobrevin is a product that contains quinine, menthyl valerate, camphor and eucalyptus oil and is marketed as an aid for smoking cessation. A Cochrane meta-analysis [90] did not identify any randomised trials with long-term follow-up. There is no evidence for assessing the efficacy of this product as an aid for smoking cessation [90].

Rimonabant

Rimonabant is a selective CB_1 cannabinoid receptor antagonist. The rationale for using this drug as an aid for smoking cessation is that it is able to restore the balance of the endocannabinoid system, which is disrupted by prolonged use of nicotine. Rimonabant also has effect in controlling the weight gain associated with smoking cessation [91].

A recent meta-analysis [92] concluded that 20 mg rimonabant may increase the odds of quitting ~1.5-fold. Moreover, rimonabant may moderate weight gain in the long term [92]. A recent multicentric randomised double-blind placebo-controlled clinical trial included 755 smokers in order to test the efficacy and safety of adding nicotine patch to rimonabant. The results of this study found that addition of nicotine patch to rimonabant increased smoking cessation rates at 24 weeks and was well tolerated, and even preserved rimonabant's reduction in post-cessation weight gain in all smokers, both those concerned about their weight gain and those not [93].

Taking all of these results into account, it can be considered that combining rimonabant and nicotine patch may be a treatment option for smokers who are concerned about weight gain after stopping smoking. However, there is current concern about the rates of depression and suicidal thoughts in people taking rimonabant for weight control. More studies are needed in order to investigate the efficacy and safety of this combination before adequate conclusions can be drawn.

Other medications

Some symptoms of nicotine withdrawal syndrome are very similar to those that can appear in hypoglycaemia crisis. This is the rationale for using oral glucose to aid smoking cessation. One trial has shown that tablets of glucose can reduce withdrawal syndrome and increase short-term abstinence rates [94].

Baclofen, a γ-aminobutyric acid receptor agonist, has been used as a pharmacological treatment for smoking cessation [95]. In addition, bromocriptine, a dopamine agonist, was shown to reduce cigarettes smoking in one trial [96].

Nicotine vaccine

Nicotine vaccine exerts its effect by blocking nicotine molecules in the bloodstream before they pass into the brain. Antibodies do not usually cross the blood–brain barrier. Studies have demonstrated that, when immunised animals are exposed to nicotine, the nicotine has no effect on neurotransmitter release in the nucleus accumbens [97].

Early phase I and phase II trials suggest that nicotine vaccines are safe and well tolerated, but the duration of effect is unclear, and the immunological response varies between recipients. In these trials, a relationship between antibody levels in serum and efficacy was noted. Higher antibody levels produced a greater efficacy. Nevertheless, it is difficult to predict which smokers will have higher antibody levels [97, 98].

Nicotine vaccines have not yet been studied in phase III trials, and the relative performance of different vaccines, alone or in combination with existing therapeutic options, is unknown.

It is known that NRT shows limited success in smoking cessation. The efficacy of nicotine may be compromised by its main metabolite, cotinine. An anti-cotinine vaccine to remove this antagonism could enhance the efficacy of NRT. In a recent study [99], it was shown that immunised animals exhibit increased serum cotinine concentrations due to sequestration of cotinine by antibodies. This increase in serum cotinine concentrations could exert some benefits in the efficacy of NRT. Further evaluation of this vaccine should be undertaken in behavioural models of nicotine addiction and relapse [99].

Summary

The main objective of using pharmacotherapies during the smoking cessation process is to alleviate withdrawal syndrome and thus to facilitate smoking abstinence.

Three medications are in common use: NRT, for which there are six different products, bupropion and varenicline. Other medications have been proven efficacious for smoking cessation but are used less frequently: nortriptyline, and clonidine. There are some other medications not currently recommended for smoking cessation: some antidepressants, mecamylamine, monoamine oxidase inhibitors, some anxiolytics, naltrexone, lobeline, silver acetate, nicobrevin, and rimonabant. Nicotine vaccine is being studied in several randomised clinical trials and is the most promising new treatment aimed at aiding smokers to quit.

NRT is the most well-studied and well-documented pharmacological approach to helping smokers to quit. This treatment acts by replacing some of the nicotine smokers would have received from their cigarettes, and, in doing so, reducing the severity of withdrawal syndrome. The last meta-analysis carried out demonstrated that the OR for abstinence with the different types of NRT compared with controls was 1.77 (95% CI 1.66–1.88).

Bupropion was the first non-nicotine medication to be licensed for smoking cessation. It is presumed that it acts on the nucleus accumbens, inhibiting neuronal reuptake of dopamine. It also inhibits neuronal reuptake of noradrenalin in the nucleus ceruleus. In 31 trials, bupropion was used as the sole pharmacotherapy and was found to double the odds of cessation (OR 1.94; 95% CI 1.72–2.19).

Varenicline is the first drug specifically developed to aid smokers quitting smoking. It acts as a selective partial agonist for the nicotinic receptor. A meta-analysis that reviewed four clinical trials found that this drug was significantly more effective than placebo for achieving continuous abstinence at the end of 1 yr of follow-up (OR 2.96; 95% CI 2.12–4.12).

Keywords: Bupropion, nicotine replacement therapy, pharmacological treatment, smoking cessation, varenicline.

References

1. Fagerström KO, Balfour D. Neuropharmacology and potential efficacy of new treatments for tobacco dependence. *Expert Opin Investig Drugs* 2006; 15: 107–116.

2. Cadoni C, Di Chiara G. Differential changes in the accumbens medial shell and core dopamine in behavioural sensitization to nicotine. *Eur J Pharmacol* 2000; 387: R23–R25.

3. Corrigall WA, Coen KM, Adamson KL. Self-administered nicotine activates the mesolimbic dopamine system through the ventral tegmental area. *Brain Res* 1994; 653: 278–284.

4. Rose JE, Behn FM, Levin ED. Role of nicotine dose and sensory cues in the regulation of smoke intake. *Pharmacol Biochem Behav* 1993; 44: 891–900.

5. Rose JE, Behn FM, Westmen EC, Johnson M. Dissociating nicotine and nonnicotine components of cigarette smoking. *Pharmacol Biochem Behav* 2000; 67: 71–81.

6. Silagy C, Lancaster T, Stead L, Mant D, Fowler G. Nicotine replacement therapy for smoking cessation. *Cochrane Database Syst Rev* 2004; Issue 3: CD000146.

7. Herrera N, Franco R, Herrera L, Partidas A, Rolando R, Fagerström KO. Nicotine gum, 2 and 4 mg, for nicotine dependence. A double-blind placebo-controlled trial within a behaviour modification support program. *Chest* 1995; 108: 447–451.

8. Paoletti P, Formai E, Maggiorelli F, *et al.* Importance of baseline cotinine plasma values in smoking cessation: results from a double blind study with nicotine patch. *Eur Respir J* 1996; 9: 643–651.

9. Fiore MC, Bailey WC, Cohen SJ, *et al.*, Clinical Practice Guideline. Treating Tobacco Use and Dependence. Rockville, US Department of Health and Human Services, Public Health Service, 2000.

10. Tønnesen P, Carrozzi L, Fagerström KO, *et al.* Smoking cessation in patients with respiratory diseases: a high priority, integral component of therapy. *Eur Respir J* 2007; 29: 390–417.

11. West R, McNeill A, Raw M. Smoking cessation guidelines for health professionals: an update. *Thorax* 2000; 55: 987–999.

12. Shiffman S, Shadel WG, Niaura R, *et al.* Efficacy of acute administration of nicotine gum in relief of cue-provoked cigarette craving. *Psychopharmacology* 2003; 166: 343–350.

13. Cohen LM, Collins FL Jr, Britt DM. The effect of chewing gum on tobacco withdrawal. *Addict Behav* 1997; 22: 769–773.

14. Shiffman S, Fant R, Buchhalter R, Girchell J, Henningfield J. Nicotine delivery systems. *Expert Opin Drug Deliv* 2005; 2: 563–577.

15. George T, O'Malley SS. Current pharmacological treatment for nicotine dependence. *Trends Pharmacol Sci* 2004; 25: 42–47.

16. Tønnessen P, Paoletti P, Gustavsson G, *et al.* Higher dosage nicotine patches increase one-year smoking cessation rates: results from the European CEASE trial. *Eur Respir J* 1999; 13: 238–246.

17. Jorenby DE, Smith SS, Fiore MC, *et al.* Varying nicotine patch dose and type of smoking cessation counseling. *JAMA* 1995; 274: 1347–1352.

18. Hughes JR, Lesmes GR, Hatsukami DK, *et al.* Are higher doses of nicotine replacement more effective for smoking cessation? *Nicotine Tob Res* 1999; 1: 169–174.

19. Benowitz NL, Zevin S, Jacob III P. Sources of variability in nicotine and cotinine levels with use of nicotine nasal spray. *Br J Clin Pharmacol* 1997; 43: 259–267.

20. Sutherland G, Stapleton JA, Russell MAH, *et al.* Randomized cotrolled trial of nasal nicotine spray in smoking cessation. *Lancet* 1992; 340: 324–329.

21. Schuh KJ, Schuh LM, Henningfield JE, Stitzer ML. Nicotine nasal spray and vapor inhaler: abuse liability assessment. *Psychopharmacology* 1997; 130: 352–361.

22. Bergström M, Nordberg A, Lunell E. Regional deposition of inhaled ^{11}C-nicotine vapour in the human airway as visualized by positron emission tomography. *Clin Pharmacol Ther* 1995; 57: 309–317.

23. Choi JE, Dresler CM, Norton MR, Strahs KR. Pharmacokinetics of a nicotine polacrilex lozenge. *Nicotine Tob Res* 2003; 5: 635–644.

24. Shiffman S, Dresler CM, Hajek P, Gilburt SJ, Targett DA, Strahs KR. Efficacy of a nicotine lozenge for smoking cessation. *Arch Intern Med* 2002; 162: 1267–1276.

25. Molander L, Lunell E. Pharmacokinetic investigation of a nicotine sublingual tablet. *Eur J Clin Pharmacol* 2001; 56: 813–819.

26. Tønnesen P, Mikkelsen K, Bremann L. Nurse-conducted smoking cessation in patients with COPD using nicotine sublingual tablets and behavioral support. *Chest* 2006; 130: 314–316.

27. Fagerström KO, Schneider NG, Lunell E. Effectiveness of nicotine patch and nicotine gum as individual *versus* combined treatments for tobacco withdrawal symptoms. *Psychopharmacology* 1993; 111: 271–277.

28. Kornitzer M, Boutsen M, Dramaix M, Thijs JK, Gusstavsson G. Combined use of nicotine patch and gum in smoking cessation: a placebo-controlled clinical trial. *Prev Med* 1995; 24: 41–47.

29. Puska P, Korhonen H, Vartiainen E. Combined use of nicotine patch and gum compared with gum alone in smoking cessation: a clinical trial in North Karelia. *Tob Control* 1995; 4: 231–235.

30. Blondal T, Frazon M, Westein A. A double blind randomized trial of nicotine nasal spray as an aid in smoking cessation. *Eur Respir J* 1997; 10: 1585–1590.

31. Jiménez-Ruiz CA, Masa F, Miravitlles M, *et al.* Smoking characteristics. Differences in attitudes and dependence between healthy smokers and smokers with COPD. *Chest* 2001; 119: 1365–1370.

32. Shahab L, Jarvis M, Britton M, *et al.* Prevalence, diagnosis and relation to tobacco dependence of chronic obstructive pulmonary disease in a nationally representative population sample. *Thorax* 2006; 61: 1043–1047.

33. Wagena EJ, Kant IJ, Huibers MJH, *et al.* Psychological distress and depressed mood in employees with asthma, chronic bronchitis or emphysema. A population-based observational study on prevalence and the relationship with smoking cigarettes. *Eur J Epidemiol* 2004; 19: 147–153.

34. Anthonisen NR, Connett JE, Kiley JP, *et al.* Effects of smoking intervention and the use of an inhaled anticholinergic bronchodilator on the rate of decline of FEV1. The Lung Health Study. *JAMA* 1994; 272: 1497–1505.

35. Tønnesen P, Mikkelsen KL. Smoking cessation with four nicotine regimes in a lung clinic. *Eur Respir J* 2000; 16: 717–722.

36. Jiménez-Ruiz C, Solano S, Alonso Viteri S, Barrueco Ferrero M, Torrecilla M, Hernández Mezquita M. Harm reduction – a treatment approach for resistant smokers with tobacco-related symptoms. *Respiration* 2002; 69: 452–455.

37. Benowitz NL, Dempsey DA. Pharmacotherapy for smoking cessation during pregnancy. *Nicotine Tob Res* 2004; 6: Suppl. 2, S189–S202.

38. Melvin CL, Gafney CA. Treating nicotine use and dependence of pregnant and parenting smokers: an update. *Nicotine Tob Res* 2004; 6: Suppl. 2, S107–S124.

39. Jiménez-Ruiz CA. Tratamiento sustitutivo con nicotina en el embarazo. [Nicotine replacement therapy during pregnancy.] *Arch Bronconeumol* 2006; 42: 404–409.

40. Ershoff DH, Ashford TH, Goldenberg RL. Helping pregnant women quit smoking: an overview. *Nicotine Tob Res* 2004; 6: Suppl. 2, S101–S106.

41. Lumley J, Oliver SS, Chamberlain C, Oakley L. Interventions for promoting smoking cessation during pregnancy. *Cochrane Database Syst Rev* 2004; Issue 4: CD001055.

42. Rayburn WF, Bogenschutz MP. Pharmacotherapy for pregnant women with addictions. *Am J Obstet Gynecol* 2004; 191: 1885–1897.

43. Coleman T, Britton J, Thornton J. Nicotine replacement therapy in pregnancy. *BMJ* 2004; 328: 965–966.

44. Lerman C, Shields PG, Wileyto EP, *et al.* Effects of dopamine transporter and receptor polymorphisms on smoking cessation in a bupropion clinical trial. *Health Psychol* 2003; 22: 541–548.

45. Cryan JF, Bruijnzeel AW, Skjei KL, Markou A. Bupropion enhances brain reward function and reverses the affective and somatic aspects of nicotine withdrawal in the rat. *Psychopharmacology (Berl)* 2003; 168: 347–358.

46. Hughes JR, Stead LF, Lancaster T. Antidepressants for smoking cessation. *Cochrane Database Syst Rev* 2007; Issue 1: CD00031.

47. Jorenby DE, Leischow SJ, Nides MA, *et al.* A controlled trial of sustained-release bupropion, a nicotine patch or both for smoking cessation. *N Engl J Med* 1999; 340: 685–691.

48. Piper ME, Federman EB, McCarthy DE, *et al.* Efficacy of bupropion alone and in combination with nicotine gum. *Nicotine Tob Res* 2007; 9: 947–954.

49. David SP, Strong DR, Munafò MR, *et al.* Bupropion efficacy for smoking cessation is influenced by the *DRD2* Taq1A polymorphism: analysis of pooled data from two clinical studies. *Nicotine Tob Res* 2007; 9: 1521–1527.

50. GlaxoSmithKline. Zyban. Sustained released tablets: product information. UK, GlaxoSmithKline, 2001.

51. Aubin HJ. Tolerability and safety of sustained-release bupropion in the management of smoking cessation. *Drugs* 2002; 62: Suppl. 2, 45–52.

52. Hays JT, Hurt RD, Rigotti NA, *et al.* Sustained-release bupropion for pharmacologic relapse prevention after smoking cessation. A randomised, controlled trial. *Ann Intern Med* 2001; 135: 423–433.

53. Wagena EJ, Knispchild PG, Huibers MJ, Wouters EF, van Schayk CP. Efficacy of bupropion and nortriptyline for smoking cessation among people at risk for or with COPD. *Arch Intern Med* 2005; 165: 2286–2292.

54. Tashkin DP, Kanner R, Bailey W, *et al.* Smoking cessation in patients with chronic obstructive pulmonary disease: a double-blind, placebo-controlled, randomised trial. *Lancet* 2001; 357: 1571–1575.

55. García-Río F, Serrano S, Mediano O, Alonso A, Villamor J. Safety profile of bupropion for chronic obstructive pulmonary disease. *Lancet* 2001; 358: 1009–1010.

56. Tapper A, McKinney SL, Nashmi R, *et al.* Nicotine activation of α4 receptors: sufficient for reward, tolerance, and sensitization. *Science* 2004; 306: 1029–1032.

57. Zierler-Brown SL, Kyle JA. Oral varenicline for smoking cessation. *Ann Pharmacother* 2007; 41: 95–99.

58. Cahill K, Stead LF, Lancaster T. Nicotine receptor partial agonist for smoking cessation. *Cochrane Database Syst Rev* 2007; Issue 1: CD006103.

59. Oncken C, Gonzales D, Nides M, *et al.* Efficacy and safety of the novel selective nicotinic acetylcholine receptor partial agonist, varenicline, for smoking cessation. *Arch Intern Med* 2006; 166: 1571–1577.

60. Nides M, Oncken C, Gonzales D, *et al.* Smoking cessation with varenicline, a selective α4β2 nicotinic receptor partial agonist. Results from a 7-week, randomized, placebo- and bupropion-controlled trial with 1-year follow-up. *Arch Intern Med* 2006; 166: 1561–1568.

61. Gonzales D, Rennard SI, Nides M, *et al.* Varenicline, an α4β2 nicotinic acetylcholine receptor partial agonist, *vs* sustained-release bupropion and placebo for smoking cessation. A randomized controlled trial. *JAMA* 2006; 296: 47–55.

62. Jorenby DE, Hays JT, Rigotti NA, *et al.* Efficacy of varenicline, an α4β2 nicotinic acetylcholine receptor partial agonist, *vs* placebo or sustained-release bupropion for smoking cessation. A randomized controlled trial. *JAMA* 2006; 296: 56–63.

63. Wu P, Wilson K, Dimoulas P, Mills EJ. Effectiveness of smoking cessation therapies: a systematic review and meta-analysis. *BMC Public Health* 2006; 11: 300.

64. Nakamura M, Oshima A, Fujimoto Y, *et al.* Efficacy and tolerability of varenicline, an α4β2 nicotinic acetylcholine receptor partial agonist, in a 12-week, randomized, placebo-controlled, dose–response study with 40-week follow-up for smoking cessation in Japanese smokers. *Clin Ther* 2007; 29: 1040–1056.

65. Tsai ST, Cho SJ, Cheng HS, *et al.* A randomized, placebo-controlled trial of varenicline, a selective α4β2 nicotinic acetylcholine receptor partial agonist, as a new therapy for smoking cessation in Asian smokers. *Clin Ther* 2007; 29: 1027–1039.

66. Fagerström KO. The effect of baseline dependence on treatment outcome of varenicline for smoking cessation, Proceedings of the 9th Annual Conference of the Society for Research on Nicotine and Tobacco Europe. 3rd–6th October, 2007. Madrid (Spain). Helping Smokers to Quit. Society for Research on Nicotine and Tobacco Europe, 2007; pp. 51–52.

67. Stapleton JA, Watson L, Spirling LI, *et al.* Varenicline in the routine treatment of tobacco dependence: a pre–post comparison with nicotine replacement therapy and a evaluation in those with mental illness. *Addiction* 2007; 103: 146–154.

68. Tonstad S, Tønnesen P, Hajek P, *et al.* Effect of maintenance therapy with varenicline on smoking cessation. A randomized controlled trial. *JAMA* 2006; 296: 64–71.

69. Willians KE, Reeves KE, Billing CB, *et al.* A double-blind study evaluating the long-term safety of varenicline for smoking cessation. *Curr Med Res Opin* 2007; 23: 793–801.

70. US Food and Drug Administration. Early Communication about an Ongoing Safety Review Varenicline (Marketed as Chantix). www.fda.gov/cder/drug/early_comm/varenicline.htm Date last updated: 20 November 2007. Date last accessed: 5 January 2008.

71. Hughes JR. Depression during tobacco abstinence. *Nicotine Tob Res* 2007; 4: 443–446.
72. Gonzales D, Jorenby DE, Arteaga C, Lee TC. Long-term abstinence is enhanced by immediate and delayed quitting with varenicline *versus* bupropion. Proceedings of the 9th Annual Conference of the Society for Research on Nicotine and Tobacco Europe. 3rd–6th October, 2007. Madrid (Spain). Helping Smokers to Quit. Society for Research on Nicotine and Tobacco Europe, 2007; pp. 53–54.
73. National Institute for Health and Clinical Excellence. Smoking Cessation – Varenicline. www.nice.org.uk/TA123 Date last updated: 25 July 2007. Date last accessed: 5 January 2008.
74. Hall SM, Reus VI, Muñoz RE, *et al.* Nortriptyline and cognitive–behavioural therapy in the treatment of ciagrette smoking. *Arch Gen Psychiatry* 1998; 55: 683–690.
75. Prochazka AV, Weaver MJ, Keller RT, Fryer GE, Licari PA, Lofaso D. A randomized trial of nortriptyline for smoking cessation. *Arch Inten Med* 1998; 158: 2035–2039.
76. Prochazka AV, Kick S, Steinbrum S, *et al.* A randomized trial of nortriptyline combined with transdermal nicotine for smoking cessation. *Arch Intern Med* 2004; 164: 2229–2233.
77. Gourlay SF, Stead LF, Benowitz N. Clonidine for smoking cessation. *Cochrane Database Syst Rev* 2004; Issue, 3: CD000058.
78. Lancaster T, Stead LF. Mecamylamine (a nicotine antagonist) for smoking cessation. *Cochrane Database Syst Rev* 2000; Issue 2: CD001009.
79. Glover ED, Laflin MT, Schuh KJ, *et al.* A randomized, controlled trial to assess the efficacy and safety of a transdermal delivery system of nicotine/mecamylamine in cigarette smokers. *Addiction* 2007; 102: 795–802.
80. Biberman R, Neumann R, Katzir I, Gerber Y. A randomized controlled trial of oral selegiline plus nicotine skin patch compared with placebo plus nicotine skin patch for smoking cessation. *Addiction* 2003; 98: 1403–1407.
81. Houtsmuller EJ, Thornton JA, Stitzer ML. Effect of selegiline (L-deprenyl) during smoking and short-term abstinence. *Psychopharmacology (Berl)* 2002; 163: 213–220.
82. George TP, Vessichio JC, Termine A, *et al.* A preliminary placebo controlled trial of selegiline hydrochloride for smoking cessation. *Biol Psychiatry* 2003; 53: 136–143.
83. Berlin I, Aubin H-J, Pedarriosse A-M, *et al.* Lazabemide, a selective, reversible monoamine oxidase B inhibitor as an aid to smoking cessation. *Addiction* 2002; 97: 1347–1354.
84. Berlin I, Saïd S, Spreux-Varoquaux O, *et al.* A reversible monoamine oxidase A inhibitor (moclobemide) facilitates smoking cessation and abstinence in heavy, dependent smokers. *Clin Pharmacol Ther* 1995; 58: 444–452.
85. West R, Hajek P. What happens to anxiety levels on giving up smoking? *Am J Psychiatry* 1997; 154: 1589–1592.
86. Hughes JR, Stead LF, Lancaster T. Anxiolytics for smoking cessation. *Cochrane Database Syst Rev* 2004; Issue 4: CD000031.
87. David S, Lancaster T, Stead LF. Opioid antagonists for smoking cessation. *Cochrane Database Syst Rev* 2006; Issue 4: CD003086.
88. Stead LF, Hughes JR. Lobeline for smoking cessation. *Cochrane Database Syst Rev* 2000; Issue 2: CD000124.
89. Lancaster T, Stead LF. Silver acetate for smoking cessation. *Cochrane Database Syst Rev* 1997; Issue 3: CD000191.
90. Stead LF, Lancaster T. Nicobrevin for smoking cessation. *Cochrane Database Syst Rev* 2006; Issue 2: CD005990.
91. Anthenelli RM. A call to action: new treatment options provide even more reasons to intervene in tobacco dependence. *Nat Clin Pract Cardiovasc Med* 2007; 4: 462–463.
92. Cahill K, Ussher M. Cannabinoid type 1 receptor antagonists (rimonabant) for smoking cessation. *Cochrane Database Syst Rev* 2007; Issue 4: CD005353.
93. Rigotti N, Chang Y, Gonzales D, Dale L, Lawrence D. Efficacy, safety and effect on weight of adding a nicotine patch to rimonabant for smoking cessation: a randomized controlled trial. Proceedings of the 9th Annual Conference of the Society for Research on Nicotine and Tobacco

Europe. 3rd–6th October, 2007. Madrid (Spain). Helping Smokers to Quit. Society for Research on Nicotine and Tobacco Europe, 2007; p. 54.

94. West R. Glucose for smoking cessation: does it have an effect? *CNS Drugs* 2001; 15: 261–265.

95. Cousins MS, Stamat HM, de Wit H. Effects of a single dose of baclofen on self-reported subjective effects and tobacco smoking. *Nicotine Tob Res* 2001; 3: 123–129.

96. Murphy MF, Hey K, Johnstone E, *et al.* Bromocriptine use is associated with decreased smoking rates. *Addict Biol* 2002; 7: 325–328.

97. Hatsukami D, Rennard S, Jorenby D. Safety and immunogenicity of a nicotine conjugate vaccine in current smokers. *Clin Pharmacol Ther* 2005; 78: 456–467. (Erratum in *Clin Pharmacol Ther* 2006; 79: 396.)

98. Heading CE. Drug evaluation: CYT-002-NicQb, a therapeutic vaccine for the treatment of nicotine addiction. *Curr Opin Investig Drugs* 2007; 8: 71–77.

99. Oliver JL, Pashmi G, Barnett P, *et al.* Development of an anti-cotinine vaccine to potentiate nicotine-based smoking cessation strategies. *Vaccine* 2007; 25: 7354–7362.

CHAPTER 11

Organising a network for smoking cessation: the role of general practitioners

G. Invernizzi*, G. Bettoncelli*, R. Boffi*, S. Nardini#

*Tobacco Control Unit, National Cancer Institute/Italian College of General Practitioners, Milan, and #Pulmonary and TB Unit, General Hospital, Vittorio Veneto, Italy.

Correspondence: S. Nardini, Pulmonary and TB Unit, General Hospital, ULSS 7, Via Forlanini, 71, 31029 Vittorio Veneto, Treviso, Italy. E-mail: snardini@qubisoft.it

The central role of general practitioners (GPs) in the implementation of quitting attempts among smokers has been long recognised [1]. During recent years, smoking cessation guidelines have been published and disseminated by medical societies on both an international and a national basis [2, 3]. Collection of information on the smoking status of each patient, administration of minimal advice and use of the five As programme have been proposed as the cornerstones of good medical practice by GPs. Nevertheless, there is still room for improvement when GPs' performance in this area is considered. Many barriers have been pointed out, such as lack of knowledge and experience in the field, shortage of time, organisation problems and fear of disrupting the doctor–patient relationship [4]. Conversely, it has been shown that smokers would rely deeply upon their doctor's advice to stop smoking, and, indeed, would like to be stimulated and supported [5]. Thus it seems that, besides motivating smokers, GPs should also be more deeply concerned and engaged [6].

GPs are accustomed to working in the usual manner of doctors, and should, likewise, apply this working practice for smoking dependence by: 1) collecting the clinical history (cumulative consumption in pack-years), and 2) using diagnostic instruments (Fagerström's and motivational questionnaires), to 3) reach a diagnosis (nicotine/psychological dependence), and 4) be able to prescribe a therapy (effective drugs/behavioural therapy).

At present, only few doctors are confident with the notion of pack-years, i.e. cumulative exposure to tobacco smoke, which can easily be calculated using the following formula: number of cigarettes smoked daily times number of years of smoking divided by 20. This provides very useful information, since the number of pack-years is strictly linked to the risk of tobacco-related diseases, namely respiratory diseases [7]. The use of questionnaires is not yet a rule in GPs' surgeries. If asthma control tests are seldom used by GPs, the Fagerström Nicotine Dependence Questionnaire and questionnaires for assessing the degree of motivation are almost completely neglected, such that it is hard to reach a correct diagnosis of the prevalence of pharmacological versus psychological dependence. It, therefore, follows that prescription of the correct therapy is very difficult. What should be done to overcome these barriers? An overview of the present status of GPs' performance reveals a landscape of professional isolation, at variance with most other medical areas, as if smoking dependence were not a medical condition, and smoking cessation not a GP's concern. Conversely, interchange with other professionals, specialists, nurses, psychologists and psychiatrists, dentists and pharmacists occurs on a daily basis.

Eur Respir Mon, 2008, 42, 98–99. Printed in UK - all rights reserved. Copyright ERS Journals Ltd 2008; European Respiratory Monograph; ISSN 1025-448x.

However, something is changing following the implementation of National Health Service (NHS) smokers' clinics. In most European countries, NHS clinics have been instituted on a local basis, and patients can be routinely addressed by GPs at a small charge or completely free of charge. This is a great opportunity for enhancing GPs' commitment and performance, provided the awareness of being part of a network grows on both sides. A few relatively simple actions may be fruitful in making the network work. 1) The NHS should recognise smoking cessation as a medical intervention, and provide smoking cessation vouchers for access to the smokers' clinics. 2) GPs should recognise their role in offering smokers primary intervention through brief advice and minimal support in the quit attempt following the five As scheme. 3) GPs are in a position to evaluate the individual risk of each smoker. In the face of smokers who need to quit urgently because of the presence of respiratory or cardiovascular diseases, diabetes, pregnancy or other conditions that can be aggravated by continued smoking, or in the case of cessation failures by recalcitrant smokers, GPs should refer their patients to the smokers' clinic with a brief accompanying letter containing a few pieces of information about the patient's medical situation and tobacco history. 4) NHS smokers' clinics should be able to take care of the patient in a reasonable time. 5) After the first visit, and at any point required during the cessation programme, the second-level NHS antismoking centre should contact GPs providing feedback concerning the ongoing situation and any drugs started. 6) If possible, e-mail feedback should be implemented. 7) GPs' collaborators (nurses and secretaries) should be informed of the network and play an active part in it. 8) Pharmacists should be an active part of the network. 9) A welcome meeting should be organised with smokers' clinic personnel, GPs, nurses and pharmacists in order to share views, problems and experience. 10) Process and performance evaluation should be scheduled on a regular basis.

Although the present authors recognise that a cessation network has a more complex architecture, including the role of academic curricula, media, industry, smoking bans, patients' associations and many other agencies, the authors would like to highlight the importance of a limited network among GPs, nurses, NHS smokers' clinics and pharmacists. If it is possible to make it work, such a network may substantially improve GPs' performance in smoking cessation, with a net increase in quit attempts and success.

References

1. Zwar NA, Richmond RL. Role of the general practitioner in smoking cessation. *Drug Alcohol Rev* 2006; 1: 21–26.
2. Tønnesen P, Carrozzi L, Fagerström KO, *et al.* Smoking cessation in patients with respiratory diseases: a high priority, integral component of therapy. *Eur Respir J* 2007; 29: 390–417.
3. Invernizzi G, Nardini S, Bettoncelli G, *et al.* L'intervento del medico di medicina generale nel controllo del fumo; raccomandazioni per un approccio ottimale al paziente fumatore. *Rassegna di Patologia dell'Apparato Respiratorio* 2002; 17: 55–70.
4. Ulbricht S, Meyer C, Schumann A, Rumpf HJ, Hapke U, John U. Provision of smoking cessation counseling by general practitioners assisted by training and screening procedure. *Patient Educ Couns* 2006; 63: 232–238.
5. McEwen A, West R, Owen L. GP prescribing of nicotine replacement and bupropion to aid smoking cessation in England and Wales. *Addiction* 2004; 11: 1470–1474.
6. McEwen A, West R, Preston A. Triggering anti-smoking advice by GPs: mode of action of an intervention stimulating smoking cessation advice by GPs. *Patient Educ Couns* 2006; 62: 89–94.
7. Cosio M, Ghezzo H, Hogg JC, *et al.* The relations between structural changes in small airways and pulmonary-function tests. *N Engl J Med* 1978; 298: 1277–1281.

CHAPTER 12

The effect of active and passive smoking on inhaled drugs in respiratory patients

G. Invernizzi*, A. Ruprecht*, P. Paredi#, R. Mazza*, C. De Marco*, R. Boffi*

*Tobacco Control Unit, National Cancer Institute/Italian College of General Practitioners, Milan, Italy.
#Respiratory Unit, Brompton Hospital, London, UK.

Correspondence: G. Invernizzi, Tobacco Control Unit, National Cancer Institute/Italian College of General Practitioners, Milan, Italy. Fax: 39 034334315; E-mail: ginverni@clavis.it

All combustion processes produce primary and secondary submicrometric aerosol particles. Primary particles are produced directly by incomplete combustion, and secondary particles are formed from gas-phase precursors. When diffused into the atmosphere, each particle is subject to different mechanisms, such as nucleation, condensation, coagulation and surface reaction, by colliding with other particulate and vapour-phase constituents, giving rise to a growth in size and reduction in the total number of particles themselves that take place simultaneously in a very short time, of the order of milliseconds [1].

Environmental tobacco smoke (ETS) is a mixture of condensate and vapour-phase pollutants (>4,000 different chemical substances), and is one of the major sources of indoor aerosol pollution [2]. The condensate phase is formed by particles whose aerodynamic profile shows a major peak in the range 0.1–0.2 μm [3]. It is acknowledged that tobacco smoke and indoor ETS pollution are a worldwide problem [4], and that a relevant percentage of people who are taking inhaled aerosol medication are current smokers (>25% of asthma and chronic obstructive pulmonary disease (COPD) patients) [5, 6]. Moreover, although inhaled corticosteroids (ICSs) are the cornerstone of asthma therapy, their efficacy is dramatically reduced in asthmatic smokers [7].

Alterations in corticosteroid metabolic pathways induced by tobacco smoke have been demonstrated at the cellular level [8]. However, no research to date has been addressed at finding a possible additional explanation for the impairment of ICS effects in smokers, i.e. the interaction between ETS and inhaled drug particles at the moment of inhaled drug actuation by the patient, resulting in a possible growth in the size distribution of the inhaled medication, which represents a critical issue regarding inhaled drug deposition and efficacy [9].

According to pharmaceutical guidelines, ICSs are studied in a clean ambient, and no concern has yet been raised about this issue [10], even though smokers take their medication in highly polluted ambient air, and resistance to ICSs has been reported as a cause of reduced asthma control in asthmatic smokers [11]. The pro-inflammatory properties of tobacco smoke and interference of smoke with glucocorticoid gene expression are considered the primary explanations [12]. However, no study to date has addressed the possible physical interactions of inhaled particles with smoke aerosol in both the airways and the environment polluted by ETS.

The aims of the present study were to: 1) evaluate the possible interactions affecting the aerodynamic profile of dry-powder fluticasone in the presence of tobacco smoke in

Eur Respir Mon, 2008, 42, 100–105. Printed in UK - all rights reserved. Copyright ERS Journals Ltd 2008; European Respiratory Monograph; ISSN 1025-448x.

an experimental setting; and 2) assess smokers' behaviour regarding cigarette smoking and timing and place of medication.

Methods

A 4-m^3 box kept at constant temperature, relative humidity and ventilation was used to analyse the aerodynamic profiles of dry-powder fluticasone (Flixotide 500) dispersed using a direct airflow of 500 L·min^{-1} for 7 min in the presence of either clean air or tobacco smoke generated by a smouldering cigarette. Particle number and classes were measured using a laser-operated instrument (Aerosol Particulate Profiler, model 9012; Metone Instruments, Grants Pass, OR, USA) with a sampling time of 20 s, capable of counting the number of particles in the size ranges 0.70–0.99, 1.00–1.99, 2.00–2.99, 3.00–3.99, 4.00–4.99 and ≥ 5.00 µm in real time. Each experiment was performed in triplicate. The background-corrected means of the particle counts in the first 80 s after dispersion of fluticasone powder were compared and submitted to statistical analysis (paired t-test).

In order to evaluate the smokers' behaviour, a self-administered questionnaire was submitted to 16 asthma and 16 COPD patients undergoing treatment with ICSs. The items regarded their current smoking status, the time between lighting a cigarette and ICS medication, the place where they actuate the medication and the possible reasons why they actuate the medication soon after having smoked

Results

In the experiments with clean air, background particles were found at a concentration of <1,000 particles L^{-1}, whereas many thousand of particles per litre were observed for the ETS background. As expected, ETS contributed to exceedingly high concentrations of particles in the submicrometric range, with a negligible contribution of particles of ≥ 3.00 µm in diameter (table 1).

When dispersed in clean air, particles sized 2.00–2.99 µm and ≥ 5.00 µm contributed ~60% of overall fluticasone particles, whereas 1.00–1.99- and 3.00–3.99-µm particles represented ~30%, and particles sized 0.70–0.99 and 4.00–4.99 µm ~10% of total dispersed fluticasone particles (fig. 1). When fluticasone powder was dispersed in the presence of cigarette smoke, a net decrease in the overall mean ± SD concentration of 0.70–0.99- and 1.00–1.99-µm particles was found, of 5,062 ± 961 and 1,979 ± 901 particles·L^{-1}, respectively, whereas an increase in the concentration of larger particles was observed compared to clean air, 1,430 ± 154 *versus* 788 ± 32, 519 ± 27 *versus* 370 ± 5, 270 ± 43 *versus* 207 ± 26 and 946 ± 154 *versus* 761 ± 53 particles·L^{-1}, respectively, for particles of 2.00–2.99, 3.00–3.99, 4.00–4.99 and ≥ 5.00 µm in diameter (p<0.01) (fig. 2). The shift towards a higher proportion of larger particles accounted for 21% of particles being ≥ 3.00 µm in the presence of ETS, as compared to 7% in clean air.

Table 1. – Background particle concentration by aerodynamic class

	0.70–0.99 µm	1.00–1.99 µm	2.00–2.99 µm	3.00–3.99 µm	4.00–4.99 µm	≥ 5.00 µm
Clean air particles L^{-1}	792 ± 19	438 ± 11	174 ± 7	26 ± 2	6 ± 1	14 ± 1
ETS particles L^{-1}	119768 ± 644	51834 ± 190	5278 ± 68	98 ± 8	168 ± 12	15 ± 2

Data are presented as mean ± SD. ETS: environmental tobacco smoke.

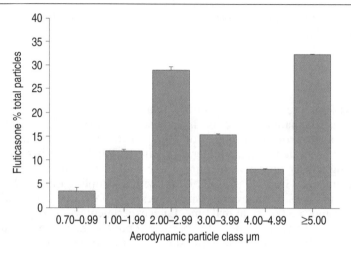

Fig. 1. – Aerodynamic profile of 500 µg fluticasone powder. Data are presented as mean ± SD.

The results of the survey regarding smoking/inhaled medication timing are reported in table 2. The questionnaire was filled in by smokers taking inhalers (n=32), 16 asthma and 16 COPD patients aged 19–76 yrs, with prevalences of heavy and moderate smokers of 37 and 63%, respectively. Most of the smokers smoked at home, and actuated the inhaler in the room in which they usually smoked. Overall, 50% of the smokers actuated the inhaler within 20 min after smoking, whereas 22% actuated it within 5 min. None of the smokers had received suggestions from their doctor regarding smoking/inhaler timing and place.

Discussion

The present data suggest that the aerodynamic particle profile of fluticasone powder can be modified by interactions with ETS-derived particles, with an ~15% increase in

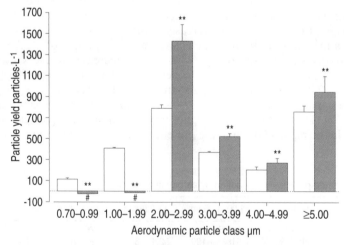

Fig. 2. – Fluticasone particle yield when dispersed in clean air (☐) or environmental tobacco smoke (■). Data are presented as mean ± SD. #: data were logarithmically transformed. **: p<0.01 (paired t-test).

Table 2. – Smokers' demographics and behaviour with respect to cigarette/inhaler timing and place

Age range yrs	19–76
Males/females n	14/18
Heavy smoker#	37
Moderate smoker¶	63
Asthma	50
COPD	50
Smoking at home	90
Inhaler actuation in room in which smoker usually smokes	100
Time between last cigarette and inhaler actuation	
5 min	22
10 min	13
20 min	15
>20 min	50
Suggestions from GPs about smoking/inhaler timing/place	0

Data are presented as percentages unless otherwise indicated. COPD: chronic obstructive pulmonary disease; GP: general practitioner. #: ≥ 20 cigarettes·day^{-1}; ¶: ≤ 20 cigarettes·day^{-1}.

particles of ≥ 3.00 µm, considered to be the threshold for particle inhalability. The concentration of tobacco smoke particles used in the present study was in the range of ETS-derived particulate pollution in the real world, but much lower than in mainstream smoke [13]. Thus the observed phenomenon should apply to both passive and active smoking. It might represent another mechanism of steroid resistance for inhaled medications in asthmatic and COPD smokers. Particle-to-particle physical interactions happen very quickly with freshly generated submicrometric combustion particles such as ETS and mainstream tobacco smoke, giving rise to aggregates of larger size. This interaction depends upon temperature, electric charge and the shape of the particles [1]. Thus interaction between mainstream and ETS submicrometric particles with particles from inhaled medications is an expected phenomenon. A similar behaviour has also been shown for hydrofluoroalkane–beclometasone submicrometric particles (data not shown). Inhaled drug particle interactions may occur not only with ETS particles present in the lung of a nonsmoker as a result of ETS-polluted ambient air but also with the extremely high concentration of submicrometric particles that reside in the lung for a few minutes after the last cigarette puff [14].

The present survey of respiratory patients who are current smokers showed that most of them take their medication in the room in which they smoke, and about one out of five within 5 min after the last cigarette puff, thus confirming the worries concerning particle interaction. The clinical impact of the interaction of inhaled medication and smoke-derived particles remains to be evaluated. However, asthmatic and COPD smokers should be advised to administer ICSs after a reasonable time after the last cigarette puff, and should take care to avoid drug inhalation in environments polluted by ETS. This advice should also be addressed to nonsmoker patients taking inhaled medications. Such hints might also apply to indoor pollutants other than tobacco smoke, and to exceptional outdoor conditions involving indoor ambient.

Summary

It has been demonstrated that ICSs are much less effective in asthmatic smokers. Most smokers are believed to take their asthma medications in the place in which they smoke, and some of them report delivering the inhaled drug just after the last cigarette puff. This behaviour raises the possibility that drug particles might interact with particulate matter present in smokers' airways due to ETS or residual tobacco smoke (mainstream tobacco smoke polluting the lung after the last puff). The conglomeration of aerosol particles is a well-known physical phenomenon that takes place very quickly and results in an increase in particle diameter. In order to verify such a possibility, the fluticasone dry powder aerodynamic profile was studied in the presence of clean air or ETS; when delivered in the presence of cigarette smoke, a 15% increase in particles sized ≥ 3.00 μm was observed compared to the aerodynamic profile of the drug in clean air. The results of the survey concerning place and timing of smoking/inhaled drug actuation showed that most smokers smoke at home, and actuate the inhaler in the room in which they have smoked. Moreover, 50% of smokers deliver the drug during the first 20 min after smoking, and 22% within 5 min after the last cigarette. None of the smokers had received suggestions from their doctor regarding smoking/inhaler timing and place. These results indicate that ICSs delivered in the presence of tobacco smoke undergo changes in aerodynamic profile, leading to a possible decrease in the percentage of respirable particles. This phenomenon could be one of the explanations for the steroid resistance demonstrated in asthmatic smokers. Smokers should be advised to actuate their ICSs after a reasonable time from their last cigarette puff, and should take care to avoid drug inhalation in environments polluted by ETS.

Keywords: Aerosol, environmental tobacco smoke, inhaled drugs, particle interaction, steroid resistance, tobacco smoking.

References

1. Lighty JS, Veranth JM, Sarofim AF. Combustion aerosols: factors governing their size and composition and implications to human health. *J Air Waste Manag Assoc* 2000; 50: 1565–1618.
2. Repace JL, Lowrey AH. Indoor air pollution, tobacco smoke, and public health. *Science* 1980; 208: 464–472.
3. Morawska L, Barron W, Hitchins J. Experimental deposition of environmental tobacco smoke submicrometer particulate matter in the human respiratory tract. *Am Ind Hyg Assoc J* 1999; 60: 334–339.
4. Smoke Free Partnership, Lifting the smokescreen. 10 reasons for a smoke free Europe. Sheffield, European Respiratory Society Journals, 2006.
5. Thomson NC, Chauduri R, Livingston E. Asthma and cigarette smoking. *Eur Respir J.* 2004; 24: 822–833.
6. Anthonisen NR, Connett JE, Murray RP. Smoking and lung function of Lung Health Study participants after 11 years. *Am J Respir Crit Care Med* 2002; 166: 675–679.

7.   Pedersen B, Dahl R, Karlstrom R, Peterson CG, Venge P. Eosinophil and neutrophil activity in asthma in a one-year trial with inhaled budesonide. The impact of smoking. *Am J Respir Crit Care Med.* 1996; 153: 1519–1529.

8.   Ito K, Lim S, Caramori G, Chung KF, Barnes PJ, Adcock IM. Cigarette smoking reduces histone deacetylase 2 expression, enhances cytokine expression, and inhibits glucocorticoid actions in alveolar macrophages. *FASEB J* 2001; 15: 1110–1112.

9.   Suarez S, Hickey AJ. Drug properties affecting aerosol behavior. *Respir Care* 2000; 45: 652–666.

10. US Department of Health and Human Services Food and Drug Administration Center for Drug Evaluation and Research, Guidance for Industry. Metered Dose Inhaler (MDI) and Dry Powder Inhaler (DPI) Drug Products. Chemistry, Manufacturing, and Controls Documentation. www.fda.gov/cder/guidance/2180dft.htm Date last updated: 8 March 2001. Date last accessed: 22 November 2008.

11. Chalmers GW, Macleod KJ, Little SA, Thomson LJ, McSharry CP, Thomson NC. Influence of cigarette smoking on inhaled corticosteroid treatment in mild asthma. *Thorax* 2002; 57: 226–230.

12. Adcock IM, Ito K, Barnes PJ. Histone deacetylation: an important mechanism in inflammatory lung diseases. *COPD* 2005; 2: 445–455.

13. Invernizzi G, Ruprecht A, Mazza R, Majno E, De Marco C, Boffi R. Real-time measurement of indoor particulate matter originating from environmental tobacco smoke: a pilot study. *Epidemiol Prev* 2002; 26: 2–6.

14. Invernizzi G, Ruprecht A, De Marco C, Paredi P, Boffi R. Residual tobacco smoke: measurement of its washout time in the lung and of its contribution to environmental tobacco smoke. *Tob Control* 2007; 16: 29–33.

CHAPTER 13

Lung cancer screening with low-dose computed tomographic scanning and smoking habits

P. Tønnesen

Correspondence: P. Tønnesen, Dept of Pulmonary Medicine, Gentofte Hospital, Nlels Andersensvej 65, 2900 Hellerup, Denmark. Fax: 45 39777693; E-mail: phtoe@geh.regionh.dk

Since the mid-1990s, several trials involving low-dose computed tomographic (CT) scanning of the thorax have been published, and there are several ongoing trials. The hypothesis of these studies is the detection of lung cancer earlier, and thus in a lower stage with a better prognosis. The overall prognosis of lung cancer is among the worst of all cancers, with a 5-yr survival of 8–10%. The participants in the above trials comprised both smokers and ex-smokers, often with a total cigarette consumption of >20–30 pack-yrs.

The prevalence of lung cancer at the initial prevalence screenings was ~0.4–3.2%, and, at the following incidence scans at 1–2-yr intervals ~0.1–1.0% [1]. This means that most participants participate in such studies for 4–6 yrs without getting diagnosed with lung cancer.

Beside the theoretical advantage of having a possible lung cancer detected earlier than otherwise, there might be many disadvantages of participation in such a screening study. Up to 25% of participants receive a message that a small nodule has been seen on CT, and that they need to be scanned again after 3 months in order to examine whether or not the nodule grows. These findings may induce psychological distress (nervousness, fear, stress and sleep disturbances), just as might screening *per se*.

Participation in a lung cancer screening programme may affect cigarette smoking in a dual manner. Some participants with normal CT scan results might be convinced that they can tolerate smoking without getting harmed and then continue their usual smoking habit, whereas others might react, on obtaining normal CT scan results, with increased motivation to attempt quitting smoking. The need for a repeat scan that subsequently gives the result of absence of lung cancer might be a motivator to quit smoking. The possibility of ex-smokers resuming smoking after a normal CT scan also exists.

Most lung cancer screening trials also contains a smoking cessation programme of varying intensity, and this may, of course, counteract the above possible negative effects on smoking of participation in such a trial. The efficacy of this smoking cessation intervention and the effect of the CT scans *per se* can be properly evaluated in controlled trials.

Trials with early detection of lung cancer with low-dose computed tomographic scans

Most of the published studies of CT lung cancer trials are nonrandomised trials without a control group. In addition, the reported quit rates are mostly self-reported,

Eur Respir Mon, 2008, 42, 106–112. Printed in UK - all rights reserved. Copyright ERS Journals Ltd 2008; European Respiratory Monograph; ISSN 1025-448x.

without any biochemical verification. This introduces a possible bias, especially if the smoking habits are reported by telephone (10–15% liars).

In a study from Ireland with no control group of MacREDMOND et al. [2], 449 voluntary participants (307 smokers) aged 56 yrs (range 50–74 yrs) were enrolled, with CT at entry and after 1 and 2 yrs. The participants had, at minimum, smoked at the age of 45 yrs and had a consumption of ≥ 10 pack-yrs (mean 53 pack-yrs), with 50% males, and were recruited by local media advertising. The prevalence of lung cancer was 0.4% at entry and the incidence rate was 1.3%. Smoking cessation advice was given at entry and at the annual follow-ups, i.e. minimal intervention. However, referral to a smoking cessation group was offered but only accepted by four (1.3%). By self-report, 59 (19.2%) smokers quit during the 2-yr period and five (1.6%) restarted smoking (table 1); 36 (8%) subjects did not attend the 2-yr follow-up.

A 1–2-yr point prevalence quit rate of 19% seems high after a minimal intervention that might induce a quit rate of a few per cent. However, this selected voluntary population might be higher in motivation to quit than the general population. The spontaneous annual quit rate in the general population is ~1–5%, and so the expected 2-yr quit rate would have been 4–6%. It is not possible to determine whether or not the CT scan per se increased the quit as there was no control group. A restart smoking rate of 1.6% seems negligible, and does not support the proposition that participants start smoking again because of normal CT scan results.

A study of OSTROFF et al. [3] reported on smoking habits in a subset of the Early Lung Cancer Action Program (ELCAP) study, i.e. 313 participants comprising 140 (45%) smokers, again with no control group. Among the smokers, 60 % were females, with a mean age of 67 yrs (range 60–84 yrs), mean use of 25 cigarettes·day^{-1} and mean cumulative consumption of 53 pack-yrs (range 10–147 pack-yrs). No formal smoking cessation was administered nor advice to quit. The exact timing of the telephone follow-up is not clear from the publication.

A total of 134 smokers were included in the analysis, and 31 (23%) had probably quit smoking after 5 yrs of follow-up, 35 (27%) had decreased their smoking and four (2.9%) had increased the number of cigarettes smoked daily. The median time to quitting after study entry was 6 months (range 1–52 months). Only 10% reported having used nicotine replacement therapy or other pharmacological aids to quitting. Predictors of smoking cessation/reduction versus no change/increased smoking were higher perceived benefits of quitting (odds ratio (OR) 4.02), greater anxiety about getting cancer (OR 2.49), younger age (OR 2.47) and abnormal CT findings (OR 1.97). Among the 66 smokers who quit or reduced smoking, 87% stated that undergoing a CT lung scan was the major incentive for reducing or quitting smoking due to: heightened awareness of the risks of smoking, fear of lung cancer detection during a follow-up scan, discussion with their physician about the radiology report, and the desire to have improved lung CT scan results at follow-up.

In a study of TOWNSEND et al. [4], 1,520 subjects, 926 (61%) smokers and 594 ex-smokers, were enrolled in a 3-yr study with annual lung CT scans with no control group. Inclusion criteria were an age of >50 yrs, and being current or ex-smokers with a

Table 1. – Self-reported changes in smoking habits after 2 yrs of lung cancer screening

	Quitters	Smokers	Ex-smokers
Entry n (%)		307 (68.4)	142 (31.6)
Change at 2 yrs n (%)/N	59 (19.2)/307[#]	5 (1.6)/142[¶]	
Total at 2 yrs n	59	253	137

[#]: smokers at entry; [¶]: ex-smokers at entry. Data from [2].

Table 2. – Annual point prevalence quit rates in a lung cancer screening trial with low-dose computed tomographic scans with no intervention for smoking cessation

	Smokers at entry n	Quitters	Smokers	Ex-smokers
Entry			926	594
1 yr	901	129 (14)	772	
2 yrs	863	193 (22)	670	
3 yrs	832	201 (24)	631	

Data are presented as absolute numbers or n (%). n=1,520. Data from [4].

cumulative consumption of >20 pack-yrs. For the 926 smokers, the mean age was 59 yrs, 50% were males, with a mean use of 25 cigarettes·day^{-1}, and they had smoked for 39 yrs. The mean±SD forced expiratory volume in one second (FEV1) was 79% of the predicted value. Most of the smokers did not receive any smoking cessation material or advice to quit, except for 171 smokers at entry. They participated in a randomised trial with minimal intervention with either written self-help material compared with a written list of Internet addresses for smoking cessation. At 1 yr, the point prevalence quit rates were 10 versus 5% (NS), although the subjects receiving Internet-based resources reported more attempts to stop (68 versus 48%; p=0.001) [5].

The annual quit rates are shown in table 2. After 3 yrs, the self-reported abstinence rate was 24%. The previous 12 months' quit rates at 1, 2 and 3 yrs of follow-up were 14, 14 and 12%.

There was an increase in quit rate parallel with increasing numbers of annual abnormal lung CT scans that resulted in extra interim control scans with an OR of 1.37 (95% confidence interval 1.12–1.67) (table 3). Other predictors of abstinence were older age and lower lung function.

Of the 594 ex-smokers, 54 had relapsed to smoking cigarettes at the 3-yr follow-up, i.e. 9.1%. For ex-smokers, abstinence correlated with a longer duration of abstinence before entry, which is shown clearly in table 4. As expected, relapse occurred more frequently among short-term abstinent subjects at entry than among long-term abstinent subjects (>12 months), with almost a third restarting smoking in the former group and only a minority in the other group, i.e. 2–3%.

The overall net result after 3 yrs was that 50% of this population were smokers compared with 61% at entry.

The annual quit rate in the general population is estimated to 5–7 % in the USA, which is higher than in most European countries, i.e. 1–3 %. The quit rate in the present study is within these ranges, and so subjects participating in a lung cancer CT scan trial seem not to experience positive impacts on their smoking habits. In contrast, the subset with abnormal lung scan results seems to quit in higher percentages, and the reason for this could be a desire to have an improved lung CT scan result at follow-up.

In a study of 154 smoking patients with early-stage nonsmall cell lung cancer, all eligible for surgery, 43% relapsed to smoking after surgery, and, after 1 yr, 37% had

Table 3. – Quit rates after 3 yrs in relation to annual lung computed tomographic scan result

Abnormal lung scans	Quitters	Smokers
0	55 (19.8)	223
1	86 (24.2)	269
2	47 (28.0)	121
3	13 (41.9)	18

Data are presented as absolute numbers or n (%). n=926 smokers. Data from [4].

Table 4. – Relapse to smoking in ex-smokers in relation to duration of abstinence at entry

	>12 months abstinence		<12 months abstinence	
	Ex-smokers	Smokers	Ex-smokers	Smokers
Entry	439	0	151	0
1 yr	418	10 (2.3)	94	48 (33.8)
2 yrs	406	12 (2.9)	102	39 (27.7)
3 yrs	387	13 (3.3)	99	41 (29.3)

Data are presented as absolute numbers or n (%).

re-started smoking, with >60% of relapses occurring during the first 2 months following surgery. There was a clear association with the duration of abstinence 3 months before surgery and prolonged abstinence at 12 months, *i.e.*, of smokers quitting 50–120 days before surgery, 60–70% were abstinent at 12 months, whereas, of subjects quitting 10–50 days before surgery, only 40–60% were abstinent at 12 months of follow-up. Other predictors of relapse were lower income, higher education (not consistent) and higher appetite score. The clinical implication of these findings could be that smoking cessation support should be delivered as soon as possible following surgery [6].

Special questions in lung computed tomographic scan trials

Validation of smoking status

The self-reporting of smoking status might be problematic since no biochemical verification was performed in these studies. Telephone follow-up, in particular, might be prone to false reporting of smoking status in order to please the engaged researchers.

Smokers attending clinic visits may be less prone to misreporting their smoking status. In a small study, urine cotinine was used for biochemical verification of the smoking status of 55 participants in a lung cancer screening trial. The participants were not aware of the purpose of the urine cotinine sample and self-reported smoking status. Of the participants, 32 were current smokers and 23 ex-smokers, three of whom used nicotine replacement therapy (one gum and two lozenge). The cotinine level was determined with a strip that changed colour. Nonsmoking status was defined by urine cotinine levels of <100 ng·mL^{-1}. Of the smokers, 30 out of 31 urine test results were positive, whereas three of the 23 nonsmokers' urine test results were positive. Excluding the three subjects that used nicotine, all 20 test results were negative. Overall, this gives a positive predictive value of 97% and negative predictive value of 100%. Thus, in this small sample, it seems that self-reported smoking status among participants in lung cancer screening trials was reliable. [7].

Adherence to protocol

In the three studies cited above, the percentages lost to follow-up were 8.0 (2 yrs), 4.0 (2–3 yrs) and 3.9 (3 yrs), which represents a very high overall adherence rate. Although dropping out seems to be a minor problem, an Italian study reported a lower adherence rate of 65% from a study of 641 individuals followed for 3 yrs. Multivariate analysis found that female sex and proximity to the centre (OR 2.33), the presence of noncalcified nodules (OR 3.35) and nursing intervention all increased adherence. Encouraging the participants to participate also increased adherence. There was a sex difference as nursing intervention had a greater impact upon females (OR 10.1), whereas abnormal lung function had a greater impact on male adherence (OR 2.09).

Attitudes towards screening

A nationwide telephone interview was conducted in the USA among 2,001 people. Several questions were asked regarding attitude and belief in screening for lung cancer. The results were presented for smokers (n=925), ex-smokers (n=517) and never-smokers (n=559) with a mean age of 55 yrs, 43% of whom were male. Current smokers were less motivated to consider lung CT scan screening for lung cancer compared with never-smokers (71 *versus* 88%) and only half of the current smokers would opt for surgery for a screen-diagnosed lung cancer [8]. The belief that early detection of lung cancer results in a good chance of surviving was lower among current smokers (49%) than among never smokers (59%) (ex-smokers 54%). Thus, overall, it seems that smokers are less interested in participation in a lung cancer screening programme than ex-smokers and never-smokers.

In another cross-sectional study, 489 current and 96 former smokers participating in a smoking cessation trial were interviewed by telephone after 12 months. Their mean age was 41 years and 65% were female. Interest in receiving information about screening was higher among current smokers than former smokers (66 *versus* 52%), and an increase in the stage of change of 1 unit increased the odds of being interested in screening by 46%, whereas every 1-unit increase in perceived risk of lung cancer increased the OR by 20%. Regarding interest in being screened, only perceived risk (1 unit) correlated with a 25% increase in interest in being screened. Overall, this means that smokers who participate in lung cancer screening trials may be motivated in a broad range of smoking cessation treatments [9].

Spirometry as a motivator for quitting smoking

These are important findings as they point to how different abnormal findings, such as lung function and biochemical risk factors, might affect the individual regarding health behaviour.

The evidence that assessment of biomedical risk could have an effect upon future smoking has been reviewed [10]. Since only eight trials could be used due to insufficient data, no firm conclusions could be drawn. However, using assessment of carbon monoxide, lung function and genetic risk of lung cancer, and ultrasonography of carotid and femoral arteries, either separately or in combination, had no effect upon abstinence rates. A recent review paper found six randomised controlled trials testing the effect of spirometry on smoking cessation, and the quit rates were significantly higher among intervention (7–39%) *versus* control groups (3–14%); however, the spirometry groups also received concomitant treatment previously demonstrated to increase cessation independently [11]. One trial included spirometry plus counselling *versus* counselling and found a nonsignificant increase of 1% in quit rate (6.5 *versus* 5.5%). Thus, overall, spirometric values seem to have a limited effect on smoking cessation. Nonetheless, spirometry is advised during baseline assessment of smokers from the general population, in order to detect lung diseases in susceptible smokers.

Conclusion

In conclusion, what is really needed are randomised lung cancer CT studies with control groups. The comparison with spontaneous quit rates in the background population is problematic since smokers volunteering in lung CT studies might differ in several points from the general population of smokers, and especially in that they might be much more motivated to quit smoking. However, overall, with the most sceptical evaluation, the quit rates in the CT studies seem to be in at least the same range as those in the general population, and probably a little higher due to a subset of more motivated smokers enrolled.

The subset with interim abnormal lung CT scan results seems to receive an enhanced drive to quit smoking due to fear of contracting lung cancer, and are probably also driven by the wish to normalise their lung CT scan. It appears that an abnormal lung CT scan result has a greater impact upon quit rates than abnormal spirometric results, probably because the latter are perceived as much less of a hazard and threat to health.

Another aspect of these lung CT scan studies might be that normal findings on scans might give the smoker the impression that it is safe to continue smoking. However, in the above studies, there was no evidence that this was the case. In one study, 20% of smokers with three normal annual lung CT scans quit smoking.

Future perspectives

In the future, implementation of the state of the art regarding smoking cessation treatment should be carried out, since only minimal intervention has been applied to date. This means that both adequate pharmacotherapy and follow-up sessions with counselling should be used. In addition, carbon monoxide measurement, as a minimum, should be used for biochemical verification of abstinence. The overall role of screening for lung cancer with low-dose CT awaits the results of the ongoing trials. However, the use of low-dose lung CT scan is already in use in daily practice for the control of small nodules found by ordinary CT scans. Such an event should also be used to deliver smoking cessation.

Summary

The present review is based on nonrandomised lung cancer CT studies without control groups since such studies are lacking. Overall, the quit rates in the CT studies seem to be in the same range as in the general population, and probably a little higher due to a subset of more motivated smokers enrolled.

The subset with interim abnormal lung CT scan results seems to receive an enhanced drive to quit smoking due to fear of contracting lung cancer, and are probably also driven by the wish to normalise their lung CT scan. It appears that an abnormal lung CT scan has a greater impact upon quit rates than abnormal spirometric results, probably because the latter are perceived as much less of a hazard and threat to health. In one study, 20% of smokers with three normal annual lung CT scans quit smoking.

There was no evidence that normal findings on scans might give the smoker the impression that it is safe to continue smoking.

Keywords: Abstinence rates, low-dose computed tomographic scanning, lung cancer, smoking, thorax.

References

1. Black C, Verteuil R, Walker S, *et al.* Population screening for lung cancer using computed tomography, is there evidence of clinical effectiveness? A systematic review of the literature. *Thorax* 2007; 62: 131–138.

2. MacRedmond R, McVey G, Costello RW, *et al.* Screening for lung cancer using low dose CT scanning: results of 2 year follow up. *Thorax* 2006; 61: 54–56.

3. Ostroff JS, Buckshee N, Manucuso CA, Yankelevitz DF, Henschke CI. Smoking cessation following CT screening for early detection of lung cancer. *Prev Med* 2001; 33: 613–621.

4. Townsend CO, Clark MM, Jett JR, *et al.* Relation between smoking cessation and receiving results from three annual spiral chest computed tomography scans for lung carcinoma screening. *Cancer* 2005; 103: 2154–2162.

5. Clark MM, Cox LS, Jett JR, *et al.* Effectiveness of smoking cessation self-help materials in a lung cancer screening population. *Lung Cancer* 2004; 44: 13–21.

6. Walker MS, Vidrine DJ, Gritz ER, *et al.* Smoking relapse during the first year after treatment for early-stage non-small-cell lung cancer. *Cancer Epidemiol Biomarkers Prev* 2006; 15: 2370–2377.

7. Studts JL, Ghate SR, Gill JL, *et al.* Validity of self-reported smoking status among participants in a lung cancer screening trial. *Cancer Epidemiol Biomarkers Prev* 2006; 15: 1825–1828.

8. Silvestri GA, Nietert PJ, Zoller J, Carter C, Bradford D. Attitudes towards screening for lung cancer among smokers and their non-smoking counterparts. *Thorax* 2007; 62: 126–130.

9. Hahn EJ, Rayens MK, Hoepnhayn C, Christian WJ. Perceived risk and interest in screening for lung cancer among current and former smokers. *Res Nurs Health* 2006; 29: 359–370.

10. Bize R, Burnand B, Mueller Y, Cornuz J. Biomedical risk assessment as an aid for smoking cessation. *Cochrane Database Syst Rev* 2005; Issue 4: CD0004705.

11. Wilt TJ, Niewohner D, Kane RL, MacDonald R, Joseph AM. Spirometry as a motivational tool to improve smoking cessation rates: a systematic review of the literature. *Nicotine Tob Res* 2007; 9: 21–31.

CHAPTER 14

Surgery and smoking cessation

P. Tønnesen

Correspondence: P. Tønnesen, Dept of Pulmonary Medicine, Gentofte Hospital, Nlels Andersensvej 65, 2900 Hellerup, Denmark. Fax: 45 39777693; E-mail: phtoe@geh.regionh.dk

Tobacco smoking has a negative influence on the outcome of surgery due to an increase in peri- and post-operative morbidity and mortality. Smokers show impaired wound healing and more post-operative infection and thromboembolic episodes. Several studies have reported that patients who stop smoking following surgery have a better prognosis than those who continue to smoke. For example, a 20-yr follow-up cohort study of 985 patients following coronary artery bypass surgery showed that patients who continued to smoke had a greater risk of death (relative risk (RR) 1.75; 95% confidence interval (CI) 1.33–2.13) and repeat revascularisation procedures (RR 1.41; 95% CI 1.02–1.94) than subjects who stopped smoking [1]. The scientific documentation regarding the efficacy and timing of pre-operative smoking cessation in relation to post-operative abstinence and complication rate is much more sparse.

The aims of the present chapter are to revise the scientific evidence regarding the efficacy of pre-operative smoking cessation programmes as regards post-operative abstinence rates and complications following surgery. In addition, smoking habits in lung cancer patients in relation to diagnosis, radiotherapy and chemotherapy are discussed.

Efficacy of pre-operative smoking cessation as regards quit rates

In a review of studies of interventions offered pre-operatively to smokers in order to promote long-term smoking cessation following surgery, only four randomised controlled trials could be found (table 1).

Only two studies had small numbers of smokers enrolled, i.e. 47 and 116, whereas the other two had adequate numbers included, i.e. 210 and 237 [2–5]. One study showed no difference in quit rates in the two groups, whereas the other three found a nonsignificant increase in quit rates. In the meta-analysis, interventions were more effective than controls 3–6 months post-operatively, with an odds ratio of 1.58 and abstinence rates of 25 versus 17% [6].

The smoking intervention was delivered from 1–14 weeks before surgery. Counselling was combined with bupropion or nicotine replacement therapy (NRT) in all trials.

Abstinence at the time of surgery was reported in five studies, and, in four of these studies, there was a significant increase in quit rates for the intervention groups (table 2) [2, 4, 5, 7, 8]. However, in three studies, the number of patients in each arm ranged 9–56. Combining the results of all of the studies, 77% were abstinent in the intervention groups versus 45% for the control groups.

In summary, each of these studies were small compared with the ~200 randomised placebo-controlled smoking cessation trials with NRT, bupropion and varenicline. The numbers of smokers in each arm of the pre-operative studies were up to 100, whereas an

Eur Respir Mon, 2008, 42, 113–120. Printed in UK - all rights reserved. Copyright ERS Journals Ltd 2008; European Respiratory Monograph; ISSN 1025-448x.

Table 1. – Long-term abstinence rates in four preoperative smoking cessation studies included in a meta-analysis

First author [Ref.]	Therapy	Follow-up months	Subjects n		Quit rate %		OR (95% CI)
			Interv	Control	Interv	Control	
MYLES [2]	Bupropion	6	14	8	21	13	1.91 (0.16–22.20)
RATNER [3]	NRT	6	56	60	18	18	0.97 (0.38–2.49)
WARNER [4]	NRT	6	93	109	31	20	1.79 (0.94–3.40)
WOLFENDEN [5]	NRT	3	105	75	22	13	1.82 (0.81–2.49)
Total		5.3	268	252	25	17	1.58 (1.02–2.45)

Interv: Intervention; OR: odds ratio; CI: confidence interval; NRT: nicotine replacement therapy. Data from [6].

adequate number is judged to be ~200. Methodological flaws appeared in many of the studies, such as counting only subjects attending the follow-ups and thereby calculating too high an abstinence rate. Taking these quality problems into account, there seems, overall, to be an increase in both the pre-operative and long-term abstinence rate of smoking cessation intervention with counselling combined with NRT or bupropion, with an increase in the odds of abstinence of up to 60% in the long term, *i.e.* 3–6 months following surgery. There is a need for a really well-powered pre-operative smoking cessation study with more intensive counselling and pharmacotherapy since surgery seems to be a window of opportunity for smoking cessation intervention.

Efficacy of pre-operative smoking cessation as regards post-operative complications

In a Cochrane meta-analysis [9], only two controlled studies were included in the analysis, and both were small, *i.e.* 120 and 57 patients (table 3). Thus the value of performing a meta-analysis was almost nonexistent. In the study of MøLLER *et al.* [7], it was planned that 120 patients undergo elective orthopaedic surgery (hip or knee alloplasty), and 52 and 56 patients underwent surgery (table 4). The post-operative complication rate was lower in the intervention group, mainly for wound infections. Pulmonary complications, requiring post-operative ventilatory support, occurred in only one patient in each group, as expected since pulmonary risk is low in hip and knee replacement.

In the small study of SøRENSEN and JORGENSEN [8], with only 60 patients undergoing colorectal resection, no difference in complications were observed as regards either all complications or tissue or wound healing.

Table 2. – Abstinence rates at time of surgery in five pre-operative smoking cessation studies

First author [Ref.]	Therapy	Subjects n		Quit rate %		OR (95% CI)
		Interv	Control	Interv	Control	
MYLES [2]	Bupropion	11	9	9	11	0.89 (0.20–3.9)
MØLLER [7]	NRT	56	52	64	8	22 (6.8–69)
SORENSEN [8]	NRT	27	30	89	13	52 (11–257)
WOLFENDEN [5]	NRT	105	75	78	51	1.9 (1.0–3.8)
WARNER [4]	NRT	117	120	69	52	2.1 (1.24–3.58)
Total		316	286	77	45	

Interv: Intervention; OR: odds ratio; CI: confidence interval; NRT: nicotine replacement therapy.

Table 3. – Effect of pre-operative smoking cessation on peri-operative complications (any complications)

First author [Ref.]	Intervention n/N	Control n/N	OR (95% CI)
MØLLER [7]	10/56	27/52	0.20 (0.08–0.48)
SORENSEN [8]	11/27	13/30	0.90 (0.31–2.58)
Total	21/83	40/82	0.37 (0.19–0.71)

OR: odds ratio; CI: confidence interval.

Another review of studies in this area identified 12 studies [10]. Five of these studies reported a lower rate of post-operative complications in former smokers than in current smokers or found no significant difference in complication rates among former and never-smokers. There was a better effect of a longer duration of pre-operative abstinence on complications. Again, the quality of the studies was varying, and, due to heterogeneity, a real meta-analysis could not be performed. An optimal period of abstinence before surgery could not be identified. Thus an estimate of the possible risk reduction could not be made. There was no increase in post-operative risks due to short-term cessation [10].

Several prospective and retrospective studies have been published as cohort studies without control groups. By performing association analysis, smoking abstinence has been evaluated as a predictor of post-operative complication rates. Some of the best of these studies are discussed below.

In one study, 200 patients underwent a coronary bypass operation [11]. Smokers that quit >2 months before surgery showed a post-operative pulmonary complication rate of 15%, *versus* 33% in smokers and 57% in those who had stopped smoking <8 weeks before surgery.

A retrospective cohort study of 288 subjects reported a relationship between duration of pre-operative smoke-free period and pulmonary complications following pulmonary surgery by reviewing medical records [12]. The rates of development of post-operative pulmonary complications in smokers (*i.e.* those smoking at least until 2 weeks before surgery), recent smokers (*i.e.* abstinence of 2–4 weeks before surgery), ex-smokers (abstinence of >4 weeks before surgery) and never-smokers are shown in table 5. These findings indicate that smoking should be stopped ≥4 weeks before surgery in order to reduce post-operative complications, taking into account that this is a retrospective study of medical records.

In a prospective study, 300 patients with lung cancer or metastatic cancer to the lung were followed after surgery [13]. Of these, 21% were nonsmokers, 62% past quitters, *i.e.* >2 months before surgery, 13% recent quitters, *i.e.* <2 months before surgery, and 4% ongoing smokers. The smoking status was self-reported, without any biochemical verification. Pulmonary complications occurred in 8, 19, 23 and 23% of the above groups, respectively. There was a difference between nonsmokers and the other groups

Table 4. – Post-operative complications in a controlled trial

	Intervention	Control	p-value
Subjects n	56	52	
All complications	18	52	0.0003
Wound complications	5	31	0.001
Cardiovascular complications	0	10	0.08
Time in orthopaedic department days	11 (7–55)	13 (8–65)	0.41
Total time in other departments days	2	49	

Data are presented as percentages or median (range) unless otherwise indicated. Data from [7].

Table 5. – Pulmonary post-operative complications following pulmonary surgery in relation to duration of smoke-free period[#]

	Never-smokers	Ex-smokers	Recent smokers	Smokers
Patients n	117	121	13	37
Age yrs	61	63	58	60
Males/females n	23/94	106/15	11/2	27/10
Cigarette consumption pack-yrs	0	48	41	52
Complications n	23	42	7	16
Complications %	20	35	54	43
OR (95% CI)	1.00	1.03 (0.47–2.26)	2.44 (0.67–8.89)	2.09 (0.83–5.25)

OR: odds ratio; CI: confidence interval. [#]: n=288. Data from [12].

(p=0.03), but not between subgroups of smokers. No difference in pulmonary complications or pneumonia was found between recent quitters and smokers.

Some studies have suggested that stopping smoking a few weeks before surgery may increase the complication rate [11, 14]. However, there is no evidence that this is the case from the present study.

Smoking habits and lung cancer

Smokers show a 20% increased risk of exhibiting radiation pneumonitis. A higher survival rate has been reported among ex-smokers *versus* smokers for patients treated with chemotherapy for both nonsmall cell carcinoma of the lung and small cell lung carcinoma. In addition, a lower rate of secondary primary lung cancers has been found in ex-smokers than in smokers.

In this group of patients, as many as 80% quit smoking during the time of diagnosis [15]. However, up to 50% of patients undergoing curative surgery for lung cancer relapse and smoke within 5 yrs, thus increasing the risk of a secondary primary lung cancer [16, 17]. In healthy smokers, a high relapse rate is observed during the first month after quit day, in contrast to cancer patients, in whom most relapses occur 1–6 months after quit day [18].

The importance of smoking cessation arises due to the decreased complication rate following surgery and during chemotherapy and radiotherapy if stopping smoking.

The period of diagnosis and therapy might elicit depressive reactions and put a heavy strain on the patient's and family's mental and social situation. Many family members of lung cancer patients are often smokers and do not quit spontaneously during this period [19]. It might also be that lung cancer patients are more nicotine-dependent [20].

It was not possible to find any published studies of randomised controlled smoking cessation studies in lung cancer patients.

Table 6. – Recommendations regarding smoking cessation for patients with lung cancer who smoke

Lung cancer patients might be more addicted to nicotine
Advice to quit smoking (lower rate of complications following surgery, radiotherapy and chemotherapy in quitters)
Administer smoking cessation counselling and NRT, bupropion SR or varenicline
Duration of therapy should be prolonged to 4–12 months according to needs
Offer smoking cessation therapy to smoking spouse/family
Reimbursement of NRT, bupropion SR or varenicline costs should be the rule
Smoking cessation service should be integrated in the clinic

NRT: nicotine replacement therapy; SR: sustained release.

Overall, this calls for a more intensive and aggressive smoking cessation effort in order to get these patients to succeed in quitting smoking. A nurse-managed programme reported an abstinence rate of 40% after 6 weeks [21]. Combination of a nicotine patch with another NRT product should be the rule, as should a longer duration of treatment with the possibility of continuing long-term with NRT.

In addition, combination of NRT and bupropion might be an option. However, since many of these dependent smokers have previously tried NRT, varenicline might be the right option for them. A post-marketing increased occurrence of depression and suicidal attempts has been reported for subjects treated with varenicline. It cannot be determined whether this is induced by varenicline *per se* or by quitting smoking. However, patients and relatives should be informed of this possible side-effect. Scheduled visits with smoking cessation counselling and support are important, eventually combined with telephone calls.

In healthy smokers, higher quit rates have been obtained if spouses are also enrolled in the same programme and quit smoking, and this might also prove to be the case for lung cancer patients.

For the small fraction of lung cancer patients with the lowest performance status, where only supportive therapy is prescribed and there is a short suspected survival time, the present author would not actively suggest smoking cessation.

Clinics working with diagnosis and therapy of lung cancer should be able to perform smoking cessation interventions, and healthcare workers should have an adequate knowledge of smoking cessation (table 6) [18]. It is important that a specific budget be allocated to each clinic for a smoking cessation service.

A weight gain of 3–6 kg for abstainers after 1 yr is found in most studies [22, 23]. In 10% of males and 13% of females, the weight increases by >14 kg, *i.e.* super-gainers. Approximately half of participants are afraid of gaining weight, and this may be a more prominent problem for females.

Weight gain can be regarded as a withdrawal symptom due to increased hunger and increased caloric intake. NRT products are only partially able to reduce the post-cessation weight gain, whereas bupropion has a little larger effect, *i.e.* a reduction in post-cessation weight gain of 2–3 kg [23].

For lung cancer patients, the increase in weight might be an advantage if they are underweight. In addition, the increase in appetite might be an advantage in patients with a decreased appetite induced by the disease *per se*, radiotherapy and/or chemotherapy.

Overall conclusions

In summary, smokers should quit ≥6–8 weeks before surgery as this decreases post-operative complications, with a reduction of ~50%. An effective programme with a long-term effect as regards cessation should include counselling and NRT, bupropion

Table 7. – Recommendations regarding smoking cessation for patients before surgery

Advice to quit smoking when patients are referred to surgery
Pulmonary physicians have a special obligation to get their patients to quit pre-operatively in order to reduce pulmonary
   post-operative complications
Less post-operative complications in quitters >2 months before surgery
Administer smoking cessation counselling and NRT, bupropion SR or varenicline
Arrange follow-up visits after surgery to enhance long-term abstinence (≥3 months after surgery)
Smoking cessation *per se* reduces overall morbidity (lung cancer, COPD and cardiovascular) and mortality
A smoking cessation service should be an integral part of pulmonary departments

NRT: nicotine replacement therapy; SR: sustained release; COPD: chronic obstructive pulmonary disease.

SR or varenicline, and seems to increase the odds of abstinence by up to 60% within 3–6 months following surgery. Smoking reduction does not seem to have an effect on post-operative morbidity. The healthcare system should offer state-of-the-art smoking cessation counselling (4–8 sessions) combined either with NRT, bupropion or varenicline for 3 months (table 7).

Surgery should be regarded as a window of opportunity for smoking cessation.

Chest physicians who refer patients for surgery for lung cancer or for other procedures in the lung should have a smoking cessation programme running in their clinic in order to adhere to the guidelines published recently by the European Respiratory Society regarding smoking cessation [24].

Areas for further research

As discussed above, many of the aforementioned studies have important methodo-logical flaws, and many studies are underpowered, retrospective and lack control groups. Calculations of quit rates are also biased as patients lost to follow-up were excluded. Adherence to the Russell standards should be the rule in new studies. In addition, the definition of post-operative complications is not always easy to understand and this might have introduced bias. Researchers should define post-operative complications before study start, and use outcome assessment that is blinded or masked to intervention assignment.

A really well-powered study would need ≥ 200–250 smokers in each arm and a 6-month follow-up after surgery. It is necessary to compare placebo with controlled administration of NRT, bupropion or varenicline for ≥ 3 months, eventually continued 1–2 months after surgery and combined with 6–8 counselling sessions.

Summary

The present chapter discusses the evidence regarding the efficacy of pre-operative smoking cessation as regards quit rates, post-operative complications and smoking habits in lung cancer patients in relation to diagnosis and radiotherapy and chemotherapy. Surprisingly few controlled studies have been published in this area, and several of the studies are underpowered and contain various methodological problems. Despite these flaws, there is evidence that adequate pre-operative smoking cessation increases quit rates peri-operatively and post-operatively, with up to 60% abstinence 3–6 months following surgery.

Smoking abstinence 6–8 weeks before surgery seems to reduce post-operative complications by up to 50%. Up to 80% of patients with lung cancer quit during the time of diagnosis, but more than half subsequently relapse. As lung cancer patients might be more nicotine-dependent and have more difficulty in stopping smoking, a more aggressive therapeutic approach should be used, *i.e.* higher doses of nicotine replacement therapy (NRT), combination of two NRT formulations, varenicline, sustained-release bupropion plus NRT, longer duration of therapy (6–12 months) and more support visits. Lower complication rates are reported in abstinent patients following radiotherapy and chemotherapy.

Keywords: Complications, lung cancer, nicotine replacement therapy, smoking cessation, surgery.

References

1. van Domburg RT, Meeter K, van Berkel DFM, Veldkamp RF, van Herwerden LA, Bogers JJC. Smoking cessation reduces mortality after coronary artery bypass surgery: a 20-year follow-up study. *J Am Coll Cardiol* 2000; 36: 878–883.

2. Myles PS, Leslie K, Angliss M, Mezzvia P, Lee L. Effectiveness of bupropion as an aid to stopping smoking before elective surgery: a randomised controlled trial. *Anaesthesia* 2004; 59: 1053–1058.

3. Ratner PA, Johnson JL, Richardson CG, *et al.* Efficacy of a smoking-cessation intervention for elective-surgical patients. *Res Nurs Health* 2004; 27: 148–161.

4. Warner DO, Patten CA, Ames SC, Offord KP, Schroeder DR. Effect of nicotine replacement therapy on stress and smoking behaviour in surgical patients. *Anesthesiology* 2005; 102: 1138–1146.

5. Wolfenden L, Wiggers J, Knight J, *et al.* A programme for reducing smoking in pre-operative surgical patients: randomised controlled trial. *Anaesthesia* 2005; 60: 172–179.

6. Zaki A, Abrishami A, Wong J, Chung F. Interventions in the preoperative clinic for long term smoking cessation: a quantitative systematic review. *Can J Anesth* 2008; 55: 11–21.

7. Moller AM, Villebro N, Pedersen T, Tonnesen H. Effect of preoperative smoking cessation on postoperative complications: a randomised clinical trial. *Lancet* 2002; 359: 114–117.

8. Sorensen LT, Jorgensen T. Short-term preoperative smoking cessation intervention does not affect postoperative complications in colorectal surgery: a randomised clinical trial. *Colorectal Dis* 2003; 5: 347–352.

9. Møller A, Villebro N. Interventions for preoperative smoking cessation. *Cochrane Database Syst Rev* 2005; Issue 3: CD002294.

10. Theadom A, Cropley M. Effects of preoperative smoking cessation on the incidence and risk of intraoperative and postoperative complications in adult smokers: a systematic review. *Tob Control* 2006; 15: 352–358.

11. Warner MA, Offord KP, Warner ME, *et al.* Role of preoperative cessation of smoking and other factors in postoperative pulmonary complications: a blinded prospective study of coronary artery bypass patients. *Mayo Clin Proc* 1989; 64: 609–616.

12. Nakagawa M, Tanaka H, Tsukuma H, Yoshihiko K. Relationship between the duration of preoperative smoke-free period and the incidence of postoperative pulmonary complications after pulmonary surgery. *Chest* 2001; 120: 705–710.

13. Barrera R, Shi W, Amar D, *et al.* Smoking and timing cessation. Impact on pulmonary complications after thoracotomy. *Chest* 2005; 127: 1977–1983.

14. Bluman LG, Mosca L, Newman N, Simon DG. Preoperative smoking habits and postoperative pulmonary complications. *Chest* 1998; 113: 883–889.

15. Sanderson Cox L, Sloan JA, Patten CA, *et al.* Smoking behaviour of 226 patients with diagnosis of stage IIIA/IIIB non-small cell lung cancer. *Psychooncology* 2002; 11: 472–478.

16. Richardson GE, Tucker MA, Venzon DJ, *et al.* Smoking cessation after successful treatment of small-cell lung cancer is associated with fewer smoking-related second primary cancers. *Ann Intern Med* 1993; 119: 383–390.

17. Kawahara M, Ushijima S, Kamimori T, *et al.* Second primary tumours in more than 2-year disease-free survivors of small-cell lung cancer in Japan: the role of smoking cessation. *Br J Cancer* 1998; 78: 409–412.

18. Gritz ER. Facillating smoking cessation in cancer patients. *Tob Control* 2000; 9: Suppl. 1, i50.

19. Solak ZA, Goksel T, Telli CG, Erdinc E. Success of a smoking cessation program among smoking relatives of patients with serious smoking-related pulmonary disorders. *Eur Addict Res* 2005; 11: 57–61.

20. Schnoll RA, Rothman RL, Newman H, *et al.* Characteristics of cancer patients entering a smoking cessation program and correlates of quit motivation: implications for the development of tobacco control programs for cancer patients. *Psyooncology* 2004; 13: 346–358.

21. Wewers ME, Jenkins L, Mignery T. A nurse-managed smoking cessation intervention during diagnostic testing in lung cancer. *Oncol Nurs Forum* 1997; 24: 1419–1422.

22. Klesges RC, Winders SE, Meyers AW. How much weight gain occurs following smoking cessation? A comparison of weight gain using both continuous and point prevalence abstainers. *J Consult Clin Psychol* 1997; 65: 286–291.

23. Hays JT, Hurt RD, Rigotti NA, *et al.* Sustained-release bupropion for pharmacologic relapse prevention after smoking cessation. A randomised, controlled trial. *Ann Intern Med* 2001; 135: 423–433.

24. Tønnesen P, Carrozzi L, Fagerström KO, *et al.* Smoking cessation in patients with respiratory diseases: a high priority, integral component of therapy. *Eur Respir J* 2007; 29: 390–417.

Statements of interest

G. Barbano. None declared. *(Author of Chapter 7)*

P. Bartsch. None declared. *(Author of Chapter 2)*

G. Bettoncelli. None declared. *(Author of Chapter 11)*

R. Boffi. None declared. *(Author of Chapters 11 and 12)*

M.C. Bressan. None declared. *(Author of Chapter 7)*

L. Carrozzi. None declared. *(Author of Chapter 1)*

C. De Marco. None declared. *(Author of Chapter 12)*

K.O. Fagerström. None declared. *(Author of Chapters 6 and 8)*

C. Gratziou. None declared. *(Author of Chapter 5)*

G. Invernizzi. None declared. *(Author of Chapters 11 and 12)*

C.A. Jiménez-Ruiz undertakes research and consultancy for manufacturers of smoking cessation medications. *(Author of Chapters 9 and 10)*

C. Lazzaro. None declared. *(Author of Chapter 4)*

R. Mazza. None declared. *(Author of Chapter 12)*

S. Nardini. None declared. *(Author of Chapters 3, 4, 7 and 11)*

P. Paredi. None declared. *(Author of Chapter 12)*

F. Pistelli. None declared. *(Author of Chapter 1)*

A. Ruprecht. None declared. *(Author of Chapter 12)*

P. Tønnesen has received fees as speaking as a member of advisory boards and research funds for smoking cessation from pharmaceutical companies (GSK, Novartis, Pfizer, Sanofi-Aventis, McNeil) producing and selling drugs for smoking cessation. *(Author of Chapters 13 and 14)*

G. Viegi. None declared. *(Author of Chapter 1)*

Previously published in the European Respiratory Monograph Series:

Monographs may be purchased from:

Publications Sales Department, Maney Publishing, Suite 1C, Joseph's Well, Hanover Walk, Leeds, LS3 1AB, UK.

Tel: 44 (0)113 2432800; Fax: 44 (0)113 3868178; E-mail: books@maney.co.uk; www.maney.co.uk

Customers in the Americas should contact: Old City Publishing Inc., 628 North 2nd Street, Philadelphia PA 19123, USA. Tel: 1 215 925 4390; Fax: 1 215 925 4371; E-mail: info@oldcitypublishing.com